Elisabeth Kübler-Ross
and
Josefina B. Magno, M.D.
President, National Hospice Organization

PRESENT

HOSPICE

A HANDBOOK FOR FAMILIES AND OTHERS FACING TERMINAL ILLNESS

James Ewens and Patricia Herrington

Bear & Company, Inc.
The Publishers of Creation-Centered Spiritualities —
Spiritualities for Personal and Social Transformation
Drawer 2860
Santa Fe, NM 87504-2860
1 (800) 932-3277

1st printing January 1983
2nd printing June, 1983

Bear & Company Books are published by Bear & Company, Inc. Its Trademark consisting of the words "Bear & Company" and the portrayal of a bear, is Registered in U.S. Patent and Trademark Office and other countries Marca Registrada Bear & Company, Inc., 6 Vista Grande Court, Santa Fe, New Mexico 87501.

PRINTED IN THE UNITED STATES OF AMERICA

Photography copyright © 1982 Don Doll, SJ

Text & Art copyright © 1982 by Bear & Company, Inc.

ISBN 0-939680-10-6

Library of Congress Card Number 82-073364

Bear & Company, Inc.
Drawer 2860
Santa Fe, New Mexico 87501

Design Execution & Text Type—David Stafford
Cover & Interior Design—William Davenport & Roger Radley
Typography—Casa Sin Nombre/Santa Fe
Printed in the United States by George Banta Company, Inc.

Chapters 32 & 33 copyright permission granted by The Institute of Society, Ethics, and Life Sciences.

Stories of Lois, Betty, John & Kay by permission Community Newspaper, Oak Creek, Wisconsin.

Excerpts from The Jerusalem Bible, copyright © 1966, by Darton, Longman and Todd, Ltd. and Doubleday and Company, Inc. Used by permission of the publisher.

HOSPICE

James Ewens and Patricia Herrington

Table of Contents

Part I: Introduction

Preface: Elisabeth Kübler-Ross   7
Foreword: Josefina B. Magno, M.D.   9
Authors' Dedication   10
Authors' Introduction   16

Part II: Hospice Care: The Way it Works   17

Chapter One: Grief as Growth: Companioning Home. An
Approach to Loss Through Meister Eckhart's Four Paths:
Gabriele Uhlein   18
Chapter Two: Sharing the Experience   24
    Cliff's Story   24
    Lois's Story   31
    Betty's Story   35
    John's Story   39
    Kay's Story   45
    A Nurse's Story   49
    A Doctor's Story   50
    A Chaplain's Story   51
Chapter Three: Reflections on the Hospice Experience   54
Chapter Four: Suggested Readings   63

Part III: The Support System   65

Chapter Five: The Support System:
    Who Provides it and How It Can Help   66
Chapter Six: The Hospice Nurse   71
Chapter Seven: Suggested Readings   73

Part IV: Children and Hospice   75

Chapter Eight: Helping Children to React to Death   76
Chapter Nine: The Phil Donahue Show   83
Chapter Ten: Home Care for a Child with Cancer   90
Chapter Eleven: Suggested Readings   97

Part V: A Vision of Hospice   99

Chapter Twelve: A Photo Essay by Don Doll, SJ   101

Part VI: The Law   121

Chapter Thirteen: Legal Considerations   122
Chapter Fourteen: How to Run Your Life When You're
     Left Alone   131
Chapter Fifteen: Coping: Insurance Need Not Lapse   134
Chapter Sixteen: Suggested Readings   137

Part VII: Funerals, Wills, and the Living   139

Chapter Seventeen: Making Funeral Arrangements   140
Chapter Eighteen: A Living Will   147
Chapter Nineteen: He Was Buried As He Wished   150
Chapter Twenty: Burying a Loved One   154
Chapter Twenty-One: Suggested Readings   166

Par VIII: Aspects of Grieving   167

Chapter Twenty-Two: Grieving   168
Chapter Twenty-Three: The Process of Grief
     For a Widow   174
Chapter Twenty-Four: A Daughter's Reflections on Her
     Father's Death   176
Chapter Twenty-Five: What Can I Say?   180
Chapter Twenty-Six: Suggested Readings   182

Part IX: New Spiritual Images   183

Chapter Twenty-Seven: Spiritual Care   184
Chapter Twenty-Eight: "L'Chaim — To Life"   201
Chapter Twenty-Nine: Suggested Readings   203

Part X: How to Begin a Hospice   205

Chapter Thirty: Information for Hospices   206
Chapter Thirty-One: A Doctor and Hospice   217
Chapter Thirty-Two: Hospice in America   222
Chapter Thirty-Three: The Evolution of a Hospice   232
Chapter Thirty-Four: Suggested Readings   244

PART I
Introduction

Preface

We have come a long way in the last two decades to help not only our dying patients, but also their families. I remember well the early years, the day-and nightlong meetings with Florence Wald, her husband, myself, and many other dedicated people, who had a dream and worked hard to make this dream come true.

We wanted to create the first American Hospice in those days, similar to the one that made Cicely Saunders known among those who cared for the dying. We had many good places in those days, like the Rose Hawthorne homes and others, all of which were founded by religious groups and worked quietly and unbeknown to the general public.

If anyone had told us in those days that we would have close to 800 similar facilities in the early eighties, I don't believe that any of the early pioneers would ever have believed it. The hard work, the utter and total dedication, tenacity, and good will and motivation have certainly born fruit!

Not all the fruit are good, and many will fall off the tree. No one should try to create fruit in a shorter time than nature has planned. It takes a loving and careful planting of the tree in good soil, a good pruning and a gentle watering of the plant. It takes a slow rooting and a spraying and then, after lovingly tendering to the young plant, a waiting for the fruit to ripen.

And so it is with the Hospices across the country. In our eagerness to make this service of love available to all terminally ill patients, we need to go slowly, to become very selective in the choosing of the sites and especially the staff. We have to put all competition and monetary or political interests aside and work in the spirit of Mother Teresa, to serve our fellow man regardless of any other issues. We have to practice UNCONDITIONAL LOVE, as an example of living and dying.

Those patients who have been cared for in this spirit will be able to talk freely about their anticipated death; they will be able to put their inner and outer houses in order and will be able to finish their unfinished business with those they will leave behind. What better way to do preventive psychiatry than to help the dying so they can teach the living!

This book contains much practical information which people may need to read before they dedicate themselves to this work. *Something Beautiful for God,* the story about Mother Teresa's work, should be added to the list of mandatory preparation. If those who consider entering this work would review their own motivation and evaluate their motives, rid themselves of their own fears, anxieties, and unfinished business, we would have less hospices in this country but many beautiful trees bearing fruit that the early pioneers of the American Hospice movement could be proud of.

I have to add with great pride and satisfaction that we have — at the time of this writing — six hospices which care for dying children. At a time when child abuse is so rampant and the number of desperate, unloved, and unwanted children is in the hundred thousands, it is important and indeed mandatory that those traumatized little ones at least get an experience of unconditional love before they die. So let us go and plant more seeds of love, more trees that may bear fruit long after we have made our own transition, so all of us involved in this work can say at the end of our days: I am leaving this troubled planet a little bit better place in which to live and to die.

Thank you for allowing me to part of this.

Elisabeth Kübler-Ross

Foreword

This book evolved out of the experiences of *Milwaukee Hospice Home Care,* and it is therefore an extremely factual and at the same time a highly exciting discussion of the hospice concept of care. By utilizing the personal accounts of hospice patients and their families, as well as those of the professional and lay members of the hospice caregivers, the authors have succeeded in depicting the "fullness of life" that is possible for the terminally ill patient who is given care by a hospice team.

The book will be an extremely valuable guide not only for families who are confronted with the imminent death of a spouse, parent, or child but for the caregivers, whether these are volunteers or paid professional or non-professional individuals. Ewens and Herrington have succeeded in covering all the details that frequently need attention to ensure that death can come peacefully, and with great dignity. It deals with two extremely important aspects of hospice care, grief and bereavement, and the spiritual care of both patient and the family members, in a very sensitive and comprehensive manner.

One of the greatest contributions that this book will make is to help families know that it is possible to care for a dying loved one at home if hospice care is available. Thus, terminal illness no longer means dying in an institution where the patient is isolated from those he/she loves at a time when he/she needs to be with them most. Hospice provides an alternative way of caring for the dying. It offers the competent, appropriate, and loving care which ensures fullness of life, not only for the patient, but for the members of his/her family.

Josefina B. Magno, M.D.
Executive Director
International Hospice Organization

Authors' Dedication

This book is dedicated to the pioneer efforts made by three women who differ in age, place of birth, religious outlook, and level of education. One began her career in Switzerland, another in India, a third in England. In a normal year they log over 600,000 miles of travel. One of them is recently married, one is a Catholic nun, and the third is divorced with two adult children. Together, over ten years' time, they have changed the attitude and perception of the world in regard to those who are dying.

Elisabeth Kübler-Ross first became widely known in America when a *Life* magazine cover story about her work appeared in November 1970. She was interviewing a 22-year-old woman who had learned only two weeks earlier that she was seriously ill. The young woman, with the *Life* reporter present, chose to talk about life, not death. She discussed her plans for a June wedding, graduation from college, and starting a family five years later.

When Dr. Ross completed the interview and thanked the young woman for coming, she responded with a lovely smile and said, "Oh, any time." The woman died shortly after the article appeared, and Kübler-Ross, looking back ten years later, said, "My own life was never the same again. I became determined to talk about death and dying until I was able to change some of the attitudes in this death-denying society."

Cicely Saunders, M.D., made her initial major impact in England, but the hospice program that she began at St. Christopher's in London in 1967 has since spread to include over 800 operative programs in the United States and Canada. She was first a nurse, then a social worker. At age 33 she returned to medical school to specialize in pain control for the terminally ill. A firm believer in the need for physicians and nurses "to give yourself with your pills," she insists that what counts most is what you let your patients tell you, not what you tell them. She asked one man what he cherished most in those who were caring for him, and he said, "For someone to look as if they're trying to understand me."

Mother Teresa is best known for her work among dying destitutes in Calcutta. She has also started orphanages for abandoned children, colonies for lepers, a free lunch program, and a house for the elderly and emotionally disturbed. When she received the Nobel Peace Prize in 1979 the committee noted that "poverty and hunger and distress also constitute a threat to peace."

Each of these three women are very direct and unassuming human beings. Kübler-Ross has said that she is not afraid to expose people to their own windstorms "so that they can look in the mirror and be pleased with the carvings of their own canyon." Of the first 800 patients that Cicely Saunders worked with at St. Christopher's, only seven could not be brought under complete pain control before they died. Mother Teresa, worried about the expense of travelling on airlines to give talks and receive awards, asked for a free pass. When her request was denied, she offered to work as a stewardess whenever she flew, so that the cost of her ticket could be used to feed the poor. When questioned about all she has achieved, Mother Teresa says, "What you can do, I cannot do, and what I can do you cannot do. Together we can do something beautiful for God."

Separate Journeys

Elisabeth Kübler-Ross, Cicely Saunders, Mother Teresa

It is important to remember that these three women have not always been so famous and well received. Each of them has struggled against institutional prejudices and has also had to contend with her own varying perceptions and interests before arriving at the prominence now given to her. Who were the people, what were the pivotal experiences that led them into the type of work they now do?

Cicely Saunders

She took up social work when a problem ended her career as a nurse, and then became a physician because she wanted to find a way to ease the pain and distress experienced by people in the final months of life. The first monetary gift towards her imagined hospice program came from a dying Jewish man who gave her $1,000 and said, "I want to be the first window in your hospice."

In her talks and writings she frequently links up ideas about pain and loneliness. Her twenty years of specialization with dying patients have made her wary of generalizations: "Some people deliberately choose not to know — they have a right to their choice and our cooperation. It's wrong to be dogmatic, and impossible to suggest a general rule. The real listener helps most of all."

With some of her patients she is gently playful, and they return the compliment. She is fond of describing a man she was saying goodbye to, for they both knew that he would not last the weekend: "Suddenly he looked up, smiled cheerfully, and said in the most matter-of-fact way, 'Any messages I can take for you, doctor?'"

She is a consummate professional who makes full use of all the weapons that psychology, pharmacology, and nursing make available to her. At the same time, she continuously tries to bring herself to each of her patients: "The dying need someone who will come to each meeting, not bearing any kind of technique, be it therapeutic, pastoral, or evangelistic, but just as another person. The person who comes to visit must be prepared to take up some of the patient's burden. Last week a woman said to me, 'When I tell my troubles to the family, I still have them just the same at the end. When I tell you, I leave some of it behind.'" Saunders began the hospice unit at St. Christopher's in 1967. There are 50 other programs in England today, and she has also been influential in the founding of hundreds of additional programs in the United States and Canada.

Elisabeth Kübler-Ross

She weighed two pounds when she was born, the first of triplets, in 1926. At five she had a severe case of pneumonia and had to be kept in an isolation unit at a hospital for many weeks. This experience convinced her of the importance for each human being to have at least one person who really cares about him or her.

She spent her first 16 years in Switzerland, while the ravages of World War II were being experienced in the countries nearby. She was 13 when she had an experience that started her actual work with the dying. She was listening to a radio newscast describing how the Nazis entered Poland. When she heard that children and old people went out to dig ditches to try to stop the onslaught of German armies into Warsaw, she made a vow she would go to Poland to help these desperate people in their hopeless task.

She kept her promise and spends her life now helping dying children and old people. In 1945, at age 19, she left her protected home environment and worked as a cook, a carpenter, a mason, and a relief worker as part of a voluntary mission of the Swiss International Voluntary Service of Peace. She worked in a variety of European countries and recalls frequently an improvised clinic in Poland in a straw-covered hut where she and other women provided patients with care and love, even though they had a minimum of medication or other medical resources. It was at this time that she was privileged to see Majdanek, the infamous concentration camp where she first experienced the gas chambers, the drawings of butterflies made by the doomed children on the walls of the barracks, and the trainloads of children's shoes that were left behind after they were murdered. This was the background, the context in which Elisabeth first conceived her lifelong work with the sick and the dying.

She continued to perform relief work in war-devastated Europe and would return to Switzerland and her family only in the wintertime. In time she studied long weeks and months to prepare herself for the very difficult entrance examination into medical school. She passed with high grades, even though she had not taken the formal college courses that were the normal type of advance preparation. Medical training was followed by specialization in psychiatry. She first came to the United States in 1958 and worked for three years in New York before going to Colorado. From there she moved to Chicago, and in the late sixties was asked by a theology student who had to write a paper on crisis in human life what topic she might suggest. Together they decided to talk with people who were facing death to see what they were going through. However, when Kübler-Ross asked other physicians in a 600-bed hospital if they had any dying patients that she might speak with, they told her that no one there was dying.

Gradually she began to meet people who were obviously aware they were dying, even though no medical person had told them about it. They also were most eager to discuss this with her. In a short while she came to be known as the "Vulture" and the "Death and Dying Lady." Her five stages — meant as a teaching tool to help people understand the roller-coaster type of emotions the dying struggle with — continue to be challenged and misunderstood by many. Fifteen years after she first described them they still remain the most concise and comprehensive schema in existence for aiding those working with the dying.

"Denial, anger, bargaining, depression, acceptance" — they are well known in this country and Europe. But Kübler-Ross takes time in her public appearances to remind her audiences that she missed all the cues with her first patient in Denver who asked her to sit down with him. She only stayed five minutes because she had to attend a meeting down the hall; when she returned half an hour later the man had died. Despite her numerous books and honorary degrees she steadfastly resists others' efforts to treat her as a distant celebrity. At week-long seminars she puts a bowl on the table during the first session and asks that anyone who addresses her as "Doctor" place $5 into the bowl. The money is then used to finance the food and drinks for the evening parties.

In recent years Ross has moved to a place called Shanti Nilaya — Final Home of Peace — in southern California. She continues to give talks and seminars on death and dying, but also focuses on helping people who are physically well to live fully in the years that lie before them. "Unfinished business" is not something that has to wait until the final weeks of life to be attended to, and both in her own life and in her seminars she is on the alert for ways to assist growth and freedom to develop before the end of life approaches.

Religiously, Kübler-Ross has journeyed along many paths. In 1970 she indicated that she was an agnostic who was uncertain either of the existence of God or of an afterlife. Today, because of her extensive contact with dying people, she is wholly convinced of both the existence of God and of an afterlife. Her lectures continue to attract thousands of people worldwide, and both the magnetism of her personality and the depth of her experiences call forth the empathy and humanity of all who hear her speak. She is a small woman, but the intensity of her style and the firmness of her conviction that people always need to have some kind of hope, even at the very end of life, is a message that carries impact in every setting and country in which she speaks.

Mother Teresa

Mother Teresa grew up in Albania in Yugoslavia, where she was born of peasant stock. She entered the convent at 18 and has never doubted since that time that this is what God wanted her to do. After a few months in Ireland studying English she went to India to begin her missionary work, spending the first 20 years living in a cloister and teaching in a high school for the daughters of the upper class in Calcutta. This was a very happy, fulfilling involvement for her and she has no feelings of guilt when she looks back on this period of her life.

In 1946, while riding on a train, she heard what she describes as "a call within a call" — God was inviting her to work with the poor. She spoke to her superior, wrote to Rome requesting permission to leave her order and begin another one, and began her work with the dying in 1952 when she came across a woman lying on the pavement outside one of Calcutta's busiest hospitals. On carrying her into the hospital Mother Teresa was told the woman's precarious condition and extreme poverty did not allow her to be admitted to that institution. Her pleading was to no avail, so she set out with the woman to another hospital. On the way there the woman died in her arms. Shortly afterwards Teresa gathered money to start a tiny house that consisted of two beds.

People living nearby complained of the smell. She went to the Calcutta Corporation and begged them to give her another place where people could die with dignity and love. They offered her a pilgrim's rest home near the temple of Kalighat — a sacred place where all Hindus desire to be cremated.

Thirty years later she and her sisters continue this same work, taking in only those that cannot be admitted into local hospitals. She has also initiated 28 homes for abandoned children, and others for lepers and the elderly. Her work is surrounded by, suffused with her faith. Those who call her a social worker are quickly reminded that she does what God asks her to do: "Christ uses me as his instrument, to unite all the people present. That's what I see happening: people coming to meet each other because of their need for God."

She does not agree with the big way of doing things, and calls her work a drop in the ocean in the suffering of humanity. To those who criticize her for merely bandaging the wounds of capitalism and doing little to change the conditions that make people poor in the first place, Mother Teresa says, "If there are people who feel God wants them to change the structures of society, that is something between them and their God. We must serve Him in whatever way we are called. I am called to help the individual; to love each poor person, not to deal with institutions."

There is one telephone and one washing machine in her convent where over 100 sisters live. She knows all of her 1,800 sisters by name, and maintains contact with them through letters she writes whenever she is travelling to give talks or visit new settlements. She is shrewdly practical, and when she received a gift of an expensive car from the pope she had it raffled off and made over $100,000 on the sale, which she then used to begin a leper colony. She believes that the greatest challenge any person faces is to find the face of God hidden in the distressing disguise of the poor. Food, shelter, and care are what the dying need, but even greater is their need for being wanted. The central part of her work has been respect for the individual human being, no matter what his or her age, religious belief, or economic status.

Most recipients of the Nobel Peace Prize are diplomats and politicians. When she received this award a reporter for the *Washington Post* wrote:

"It is the example of personal devotion to these destitute people, as individuals, that is compelling. The award is, among other things, a reminder of a kind of poverty that most Europeans and Americans are unlikely ever to see. Occasionally the Nobel Committee uses the prize to remind the world that there is more than one kind of peace, and that politics is not the only way to pursue it."

It is difficult to overestimate the impact that these three women have made worldwide on behalf of the sick and dying. Their awards encompass all major honors bestowed by private citizens and governments. None of them charge for the work they do, and yet each has ample sources of funds given by people who wish to advance their unique charities. More importantly, because they have travelled down the unique paths that their lives have opened to them, they have advanced the frontiers of the world in regard to the needs of the dying. As a result, people alive today can approach the mystery of their own death with an assurance that all aspects — physical, emotional, and spiritual — will be attended to with the utmost sensitivity and concern. This handbook is dedicated to these three women, in grateful recognition for their superb achievements.

Authors' Introduction

This handbook is fashioned to meet the needs of families facing the death of a loved one. It contains practical information on home nursing care, legal matters, how to help children, and making funeral arrangements. It also has articles describing families who were able to care for a member of their family at home during the final months of life.

The need for such a work was first expressed by the families our hospice home care program was dealing with. The questions they asked and the experiences they had led our staff to begin to write down the central issues that arise at this crucial time in a family's existence. We made it a point to ask our families what helped them most during the time of care and who was important to them as they worked through the period of grieving. Their responses are included in the following pages.

Fifty years ago most people died in the context of their own homes. That option has become a reality for families today because of the growth of the hospice movement in the United States and England. Three women have been influential in this new approach to care for the dying, Elisabeth Kübler-Ross, Cicely Saunders, and Mother Teresa. This handbook is dedicated to them and the revolution they have brought about for the needs of the dying across the world.

Our gratitude to their vision and courage is immense. We are also grateful to the families who have given us the privilege to enter their homes and share their lives at a time of great urgency and need. We were a small staff, a new health care program that grew slowly, with limited funds, to assist families in caring for their loved ones in their own homes. The love and depth of concern that we have seen expressed far outweigh the sadness that this involvement necessarily entails.

Finally, we would like to acknowledge the cooperation provided by the members of the Milwaukee Hospice Home Care Staff in the writing of this book. They include: Kathy Dahlk, M.S.W., Alice Hardaker, R.N., and Kathie Harrison, R.N., John Hurley, M.D., and Mary New, Support Staff.

Others whose contributions have been significant are: John Conway, Dolores Gencuski, and Erica John.

May the content of this book serve as a source of hope for families. In particular, may it commemorate the patients who have worked with our staff and their families who continue to grow because of the life we shared in together during their final days on earth.

James Ewens
Patricia Herrington

*

PART II
Hospice Care: The Way It Works

Can there be meaning and hope in the face of death? Can we still trust in the unconditional meaningfulness of life despite its apparent collapse into nothingness? Death in an obvious sense refers to the bodily break-up which inevitably and relentlessly comes to all persons. It is the end of all vital functions and of the distinctly human activity and relationships in the world. It is the cold fact which remains seemingly outside our freedom of choice.

We may encounter death in a cruel and violent fashion as something inflicted, such as slaughters in concentration camps, slayings in armed combat, or the ravages of starvation. Yet dying alone in the possibly impersonal atmosphere of a large public hospital can have its own terrors. We might prefer to meet death in a familiar setting, surrounded by family and friends. When facing death we seem to seek the most supportive situation.

The first article in this section deals with death as companioning home, as seen from the four paths of Meister Eckhart, which provide the setting and context for "how hospice works."

There are many ways to describe the components of hospice care. Definitions, lists of staff duties and disciplines, statistical data — all can provide some of the information needed. But the simplest and most direct way is to describe how individuals families have experienced this care.

CHAPTER ONE

Grief as Growth: Companioning Home

An Approach to Loss Through
Meister Eckhart's Four Paths

Grieving

It has been said that we fear not death, but rather the incompleteness of our lives. It is loss that is grieved. Yet sooner or later, the experience of a deep loss, the experience of the death of a loved one is a part of life, as is the knowledge of the surety of our own death. Ironically, grief in the face of such experiences is seldom understood as something to be fully lived and treasured. It is seldom understood as a natural process that initiates change. Grief is the normal, universal response to loss. It is a powerful emotional reaction often resulting in helplessness, loss of control, anger, despair, and loneliness. To be at ease with the ordinariness and naturalness of the experience is the catalyst for strength, growth, and transformation.

Unfortunately, grief is not often frankly discussed in the light of this mysterious potential. Goethe once reflected that the German word for mystery, "Geheimnis," is derived from "Heim," which means home. This is interesting to ponder—that we find "home" in the core of mystery. Dying is perhaps the greatest mystery we face. But what consolation and confirmation can we find in this "homecoming"? Churches often deal only with "afterlife." The stark reality of the dying process is seldom dealt with. Perhaps it is that we have forgotten how to be at home in our full bodily reality. It is a reality in which death is the final, consummate mystery.

Healthy spiritual traditions understand this necessary loss/grief process very well. The paradigm of death/

rebirth is a common theme in these traditions. They deal with the total fullness of life and are capable of embracing the completeness of body and psyche. They provide not a series of dogmas, but rather a definition of an organic approach that provides a way of dealing with and integrating all the events of our lives.

Specifically, the spirituality of Meister Eckhart offers just such an understanding. It embodies the very ordinariness of letting go, of dying. It celebrates the creative birthing of a transforming newness that springs from a trust of the emptying process. It begins with the naming and blessing of that which simply is. It demands a sinking into the vortex of the experience that results in a creative breakthrough. It allows for new life responses; it allows for redefinition and growth.

The hallmark of this spirituality is its cyclic nature. It is a cycle of unending transformation. The moment we have redefined ourselves and our life responses, the movement is to yet another letting go. Thus the living process continues. Every new birth carries within it the seed of its own death and transformation. It is a constant call to ever new, ever richer being, ever fuller living.

This is particularly helpful in understanding the grieving process itself. It is the survival of the necessary pain that brings us to the treasuring of this circle of growth. A word of caution, however, is in order here. The circle of transformation is unique to each individual. There are generalizations that can be drawn as guidelines, but only with the understanding that they are merely reference points on a continual wheel of growth. Each phase, then, is to be entered into fully, and is not to be rushed through in order to achieve "acceptance." Likewise it is crucial to remember that further change is already inherent in acceptance, and that acceptance is individually different.

In the grieving process these points of reference can be

understood as a four-fold pattern that corresponds to the Four Paths of Meister Eckhart's spiritual journey:
1. The experience of the loss; the naming and recognition of this event.
2. The entering into the experience; the falling into the pain of it; the letting go of what was.
3. The response to the pain; the creating from the experience; the trusting of one's images (this is the breakthrough into a new reality, a new naming of self.)
4. The newly birthed identity in action; responding from the new image of self.

Surviving the necessary pain.

Given this four-fold understanding of the grieving process, there emerge specific strategies of intervention. Again, it is important to understand that grief is normal and not maladaptive. It is a part of the human condition. It is shared by all. Grief and support that are effective recognize this. It is not a desire to "take the suffering away," but rather it is a companioning, a special sense of being "at home" with the mystery of letting go, and a desire to share in another's painful growth.

This companioning presupposes an understanding of what is generally appropriate inthis four-part cycle:

1. The name of the loss.

This is characterized by the onset of the crisis. There is a stunned reaction and a numbness that may last for a period of weeks. The grieving person exhibits a certain flatness of feeling and mechanically completes tasks amid a sense of hopeless helplessness. It is as if he or she were anesthetized to the pain, and all that is possible is the naming of the grief.

The temptation here is for the help-giver either to laud the bereaved's apparent stoicism or to be dismayed at the lack of emotion that is displayed. In reality, this dullness of affect allows for the carrying out of important rituals, and it insulates against pain that would be initially overwhelming.

2. The acute ventilation of pain.

When a person is ready, there follows a period of three to five days during which intense feelings are experienced. Glib reassurances that "everything will be all right," or that one understands "exactly" how the grieving person feels, are of little use here. There is a low tolerance for intellectualization or discussion. Normal activities cease as the person falls into the full pain of grief.

Here is it crucial to remember that this experience is idiosyncratic, that indeed no one can understand what the grieving person is "really" feeling. Equally key is to have no expectations as to what form the expression of the pain will take. Anger, panic, guilt, and loneliness, are natural, as are self-absorbtion and shame. What is needed is encouragement in trusting the experience and honoring the individual uniqueness of its expression. Helpful, too, is verbalized acknowledgement that we are limited in our understanding of the grieving person's experience, but that we are ready to be attentive and supportive of his or her touching of pain. It is the person's trust of his or her experience as unique and valid that will allow for his or her creative reorganization and growth.

3. Breakthrough.

This is a time of reorganizational convalescence, approximately four to six weeks in duration. Having entered into the pain, the person needs to creatively respond. Persons choose, at this time, to remember specifically those events that place emphasis upon the pain of the situation. There is the expression of much anger and other related feelings. There is much dream activity and the manisfestation of all manner of physical symptoms. Further, there might well be "bizarre" delusions, such as the hearing of voices, etc. These are all, literally, attempts to "do something" about the pain.

As can be anticipated, then, the need to talk usually increases significantly. This is how the grieving person can affirm reality and actualize the loss. What is required is a facilitation of this curative storytelling, over and over again, until the new image of the now-changed self can be trusted and hope breaks through.

4. Responding from the newly affirmed reality.

The reality that is affirmed in this rehabilitative time is that indeed loss has occurred and as a result the grieving person is changed. It is a period that may last well up to two years, depending upon the trauma and significance of the loss. During this time it is vital that the new reality of the individual as a changed person is affirmed. Positive acceptance of the person is crucial.

Also at this time the grieving person will begin to articulate a fuller memory. There is a reorganization of the past and of the future to include joys as well as sorrows. Thus it is helpful to assist and affirm the remembrance of experiences before the loss, and the anticipation of those yet to occur. It is a re-establishing of a reality that allows a person to fully be his or her changed self.

It is important that the help-giver not limit this growth by preconceived expectations of what this transformation should be like. Again, the respect for the uniqueness of the person is of paramount importance.

Companioning home.

Clearly, the stance of help-giver to grieving persons is one of sharing the human condition. What is required is compassionate presence, the understanding that we are mutually mortal. We are pilgrims together in the face of change and growth. Of the labor of this companioning, strength is birthed. Eckhart would counsel us to begin with the heart. Our caring hearts would then lead us on a path that is most familiar. It is a path that takes us deeply into the heart of painful mystery. Yet as we accompany each other home there, our lives are the fuller for it. And, we have the treasure of our new selves to show for it.

Gabriele Uhlein

References

Fox, Matthew. "Meister Eckhart on the Four-Fold Path of a Creation-Centered Spiritual Journey," in Matthew Fox, ed., Western Spirituality: Historical Roots, Ecumenical Routes. Santa Fe: Bear & Co., 1981, pp. 215-248.

Henderson, Stephen. Facing Life Through Death. Virginia: Full Circle, 1976.

Nouwen, Henri. The Wounded Healer. New York: Doubleday, 1972.

Weisman, Avery. On Dying and Denying. New York: Behavioral Publications, 1972.

CHAPTER TWO

Sharing the Experience

The following pages detail how individual persons dealt with the loss of a central family member. These descriptions are followed by comments made by members of the hospice staff and practical suggestions that families have sent in after caring for a loved one at home.

Cliff's Story

When Cliff left Deaconess Hospital in January 1979, after a series of chemotherapy and radiation treatments for stomach cancer, he had had enough of hospitals.

He was only 39 years old. He had a wife and two young daughters. He knew that this illness, diagnosed almost four years earlier, was terminal. In fact, he came near death during his hospital stay.

So when he went home, he and his wife, Yvonne, decided he would stay there.

And he did. Cliff died at home on the day after Thanksgiving.

He might not have been able to stick with his decision had it not been for a new organization called the Milwaukee Hospice.

The hospice concept—the idea of a place that provides care for the dying—is still relatively new. Much has been written about it in the past few years, and two area hospitals, St. Joseph's and Rogers Memorial in Oconomowoc, have established hospices within their walls.

The Milwaukee Hospice, which went into operation in

May of 1979, is different. It's not a place, but a group of people who are dedicated to helping dying persons who decide to remain at home.

Cliff and Yvonne learned about the Milwaukee Hospice from their doctor. (Yvonne asked that her last name not be used. Widowhood has made her aware of a new vulnerability—that of the woman alone with two young children.)

They had some misgivings about the hospice idea. "My husband was kind of skeptical," said Yvonne as she recalled their experience in a recent interview. "We didn't know that much about it. But then Alice came to see us. I would say her personality is what made Cliff decide to go ahead with it."

Alice is Alice Prochniewski, a registered nurse who has worked for years with the dying in hospitals. That work has convinced her that "There ought to be a better way," as she puts it. "People ought to be able to die with support and not be abandoned when treatment fails," she says. "Dying patients tend not to get the attention they need."

Ms. Prochniewski began visiting Cliff and Yvonne at their Muskego home in late August, stopping in about every two weeks at first. Cliff was still up and around and able to take medication on his own. During the summer he had felt well enough to go camping with the family and go fishing occasionally.

As he began to fail, Ms. Prochniewski called on him every week. During their conversations she answered all the questions that preyed on Cliff's mind. She talked with Yvonne, too, about caring for Cliff. Knowing that she was always accessible by telephone was a great comfort, Yvonne said.

Hospice staff members carry beepers, so that they can be reached in an emergency.

For Cliff, staying home was far more comfortable than being in the hospital. "He didn't like the whole hospital atmosphere—doctors and interns coming in and out, examining him," said Yvonne. Also, he enjoyed having friends around. Even though he was ill, Cliff liked to have friends drop by to talk. That sort of visiting was easier at home.

Having Cliff at home was also easier on Yvonne. Last winter, when he was in the hospital, was a horror for her. Their home is 20 miles southwest of Milwaukee, and heavy snowfalls sometimes made it impossible for her to get into town to see Cliff, even when he was so low there was fear he wouldn't make it.

At home, they set up a hospital bed in the dining room so that Cliff could be close to Yvonne as she worked in the kitchen. During the last week of his life, his need to have her near increased. "He didn't even want me to go downstairs to the basement to wash clothes," she said.

Even so, the decision to stay home was not easy to stick with. About two weeks before he died, Cliff said he wanted to go back into the hospital.

"He was afraid of being so sick it would be embarrassing to the children and me. He said, 'I'm afraid I'm going to be a burden to you.' He kept saying he was afraid he would get 'messy sick.' I told him I didn't want him back in the hospital. I wanted him here," said Yvonne.

Another common fear about staying at home centers on the idea that in a hospital something could be done to improve or prolong life. Cliff felt this way at one point, and called his doctor. The doctor reassured him that, much as he would like to do so, there was nothing more he could do for Cliff.

Finally, there is the question of pain. The fear of pain is probably the first thing that comes to mind when people think of a prolonged death. Indeed, pain control is the most important element of care for the dying, says Father James Ewens, Milwaukee Hospice director.

"You've got to control pain or it makes no difference where they are," he said in an interview at the hospice office at 1022 N. 9th St. "We had heard it was possible to control pain in 80% to 85% of the cases. That sounds high, but it has proved true. We can control pain just about all the time."

The key is to give medication regularly, every three or four hours, rather than after the pain returns. That attitude is sometimes a difficult one for hospitals and doctors, Ewens said, because they are oriented toward cure.

"It's difficult for doctors to shift gears," he said. "They are legitimately concerned about hooking patients on drugs. Imagine a doctor walking down the hospital hall. He visits nine patients who are going to get well and the tenth is dying. It's just difficult to shift gears."

Cliff had little problem with pain control, Yvonne said. In fact, in the final week of his life, when he slept most of the time, he seemed to move beyond pain. "He kept saying, 'I feel good,' " she said.

If Cliff had insisted on returning to the hospital, the hospice staff would have supported him in his decision, Ewens said. "It doesn't work for all. If a person wants to die at home, that's fine. If he wants to go into the hospital, that's fine, too," he said.

The hospice gives more than physical care—it provides emotional and practical support, too. Ms. Prochniewski helped Cliff prepare for his death in several ways. She encouraged him to make out a will and plan his funeral, which he did, and when he talked about religious questions, she listened sympathetically. Ewens came out weekly to visit and he, too, talked with Cliff and prayed with him. The fact that Ewens is a Jesuit priest and the couple were Lutheran made no difference. The hospice is not affiliated with any religious institution.

"It was a search for God," Yvonne said. "I would read Bible passages for him. He looked forward to Father Ewens and our pastor also visited."

The need to work through the search for God seemed to keep Cliff alive that last week, Yvonne said. "Alice was amazed at his willpower. He told her, 'I have this puzzle to put together. I can see the door. It's dark, and I don't know what's on the other side.'"

Cliff began to fail badly the Sunday before Thanksgiving, and took to his bed. By Thanksgiving Day he was unresponsive, but at the end of the day, he was able to say, "I didn't spoil Thanksgiving." He had been worried about that, Yvonne said.

That night he suddenly had a surge of energy and alertness. "He actually sat up in bed," said Yvonne. "He said, 'Let's pray together.' We said the Lord's Prayer together, and then he said, 'I feel as though the Lord is standing right next to my bed.' People talk about miracles," said Yvonne, "Well, I think that was a miracle."

Cliff went into a coma after that. He died the next afternoon with Yvonne and Ms. Prochniewski at his side.

The couple's two daughters, Stacy, 11, and Jamie, 9, were at home when their father died. They were in the living room with an aunt who was keeping them busy at quiet games.

There are superstitions about death in a home, but Yvonne doesn't share them. "We have no fears at all about him dying here," she said. "Before Cliff died, the girls were watching a movie and they got some ideas.

Stacy said to me, 'Mama, are we going to be haunted if Daddy dies here?' I told them to talk to their dad about that. He said, 'Do you think I'd haunt you?' They said no. That put an end to their fears."

The girls expressed other feelings, too. One day Stacy burst out with, "Sometimes I wish Daddy would die so he'd be through suffering," Yvonne recalled.

"She had the guiltiest look on her face after she said it," said Yvonne. "I told her not to feel guilty, that I had felt that way a couple of months ago and when I told Alice about it, she said it was a normal way to feel."

Ms. Prochniewski became such a part of the family that the girls began to call her "Auntie Alice." Her involvement didn't end with Cliff's death. She pronounced him dead (a doctor signed the death certificate later), attended the wake, and continues to call and drop in on the family. When Yvonne had a birthday in January, "Auntie Alice" showed up with a pizza, ice cream, and cake.

Ewens stays in touch, too, because he knows the grieving process takes much longer than most people expect.

Families who have kept a dying member at home may feel at first that they have worked through their grieving before the person dies, hospice social worker Kathy Dahlk observed.

"Some people think they've done all that—a sort of anticipatory grieving—before the death. They don't expect to grieve so much after," she said. Caring for the dying at home can ease some of the guilt and sense of helplessness families often experience when a family member dies.

The Milwaukee Hospice is making some inroads into the cost of dying, too. "In terms of cutting cost, this is much, much cheaper than any other way," said Ewens. Compared with the expense of hospital care, Ewens estimates a savings of $200 to $300 a day.

In spite of this cost reduction, the hospice finances are tight. Medicare will not pay for in-home hospice care because insurance companies here interpret it as maintenance level care (this is not true in all states). Under Wisconsin's mandated benefits law, private insurance does reimburse for in-home hospice nursing care for people under 65, but other services the hospices provides are not reimbursed.

The Milwaukee Hospice has three main funding sources, insurance reimbursements, memorials from the families and friends of the deceased, and various local foundation grants.

When a family decides to keep a dying member at home, they take on a big responsibility, but with that goes a great deal of control over the dying process. The family itself becomes the primary caregiver. Doctors and nurses are secondary.

"Once you put care in the home, every role changes," Ewens observed. "The nurse becomes the main support and teacher of care. The physician is a backup to the nurse and is no longer the primary person in the care," he said.

The hospice also makes use of friends and neighbors. "We find out who are the people the family already knows, the people who call up and say, "What can I do?" continued Ewens. "Sometimes it is hard for the family to do things like wash clothes. We can ask, WE can do that." If necessary, the hospice calls in its own volunteers to help with household chores.

Relying on people the family already knows and feels comfortable with is far preferable to calling in strangers, Ewens said. "It is important not to have too new people coming in. The family wants to maintain its privacy and sense of continuity. If too many people are involved, you lose that. But if we support the family efforts, they don't need that much help," Ewens said.

Reprinted with permission from the Milwaukee Journal.

Lois' Story

"I would do it over again, the same way," Jack Michel said thoughtfully, and it is apparent he is a man at peace. Jack lost his wife, Lois, on December 7. He and his seven children cared for her during her final days right in their own home, with the same close family spirit sustaining them that they have always shared.

During the last year of Lois' life, she spent a lot of time in the hospital. There were hospitalizations for brain surgeries as well as an operation to repair a broken hip. There was therapy, and she received 33 daily cancer treatments as an outpatient. In all she spent] 2 weeks of the year in the hospital.

The family had praise for the cancer floor at St. Joseph's Hospital. "They were extremely nice," Jack said. "The kids could spend a lot of time at the hospital." Both Jack and Kathy, one of his oldest daughters, talked about how skillful the nurses were in dealing with problems like theirs and how relaxed the atmosphere was.

"My brother's dog had puppies while Mom was there," Kathy said, "and they let him bring all the puppies to the hospital. It was very relaxed, but it wasn't home."

In the fall, when Lois had been back home again for while, she began to get weaker. The hip fracture in September had set her back. Visiting Nurses were making visits twice a week to check on her, take blood pressure, and do physical therapy.

The family rented a wheelchair and she was up a good

part of each day. She ate all her meals at the table, which meant a lot to her and to all the family. "She could guide us," Kathy said. "She could tell us what to do. She could still be a mother."

Then along about the first of November, "My wife was really down," Jack said. "Her morale was low. The doctor who was doctoring her was wonderful and she wanted to call him to come out."

Even though Jack knew that medically everything had been done for his wife, he wanted the visit, too, for her peace of mind. He talked with the doctor about the hospice facility at St. Joseph's which they had discussed before.

With the realization that there might not be much time left, the doctor also told Jack about the Milwaukee Hospice program for home care.

It was time for Jack to talk to his family. It is their habit to talk things over together when there are serious decisions to be made.

Four of the children are old enough to be living away from home but all live fairly close to the family homestead. The three youngest—Diane, 11, Bobby, 16, and Jackie, 18—still live at home. They all agreed they would like to do whatever it took to keep Mom at home.

"My main concern was for the family and for her," Jack said. "I wanted her to have the best care possible. I really didn't know how it would work. I wasn't at all sure about her ending days, if she might have suffering."

They called Milwaukee Hospice, and Father Jim, as the family quickly came to know him, came out. Father Jim is James Ewens, chaplain-director of Milwaukee Hospice, which is not formally affiliated with any particular religious denomination.

Ewens explained how the Hospice home care program could help. He felt the family was capable of doing what they were choosing to do with the help of some visits from the professional staff. He assured Jack that if at any time Lois needed more care than she could get at home, different arrangements could be made.

He also told them that financial consideration should be the last thing to worry about. Hospice services are provided according to need rather than ability to pay. Some insurance companies pay for nursing visits, but, when insurance is not available, charges are made on a sliding scale based on income.

Nurses came in three times a week. "They were never in a hurry," Jack said. They bathed and massaged her. They taught the family how to move her from hospital bed to wheelchair so they could continue to have meals together.

Bobby said, "It was nice to know you could come out of your room and Mom was there."

The nurses and Ewens's frequent visits helped the whole family. "They helped with the physical and gave emotional support," Kathy said. Talks with the nurses helped them handle things that came up and helped them know what to expect. "Father Jim talked with Mom. He would have a meal and talk with the whole family. He had a way of talking with each person, one on one, talking about anything."

Although each family member found his own way to help, they decided one of them needed to be there full time. Daughter Judy, 20, lived the furthest away and was attending college. She found it hard to be away and was unsure of her future personal goals. Judy dropped out of school to be available for her mother's daytime care.

Since Jack is a salesman, it is necessary for him to do some travelling. "When I travelled, Kathy came to stay," Jack said. When he was home he spent nights sleeping on the couch close to his wife's hospital bed. A few nights he didn't get any sleep. But his wife would sit at the edge of the bed and fall asleep in his arms.

Just before Thanksgiving, a priest friend of the family came and offered a family mass in their home and anointed Lois. She was getting weaker but it was still important to her to be with and say things to her family.

"It was hard to understand her sometimes when she could just whisper. But Diane could often understand. They were close buddies," Kathy said. "And Mom never lost her sense of humor. She had a neat sense of humor."

Being together during these final weeks changed the family's ideas about death. "It makes you feel good to know you did the best you could," Jack said, "and to be able to spend as much time as possible together."

Kathy and Jack both felt that the opportunities for time just can't be the same in the hospital. "It's good to know you did everything and said everything," Kathy said.

They believe this time together helps to deal with the reality of death. "Even though we all miss her a lot, death does not seem so horrible now. It is not such a frightening thing anymore, especially when you believe in life after death."

During those final weeks of illness and in the days after Lois died, the Michels couldn't believe all the thoughtful things their friends thought of doing for them. "It amazed me," Jack said. "People were really wonderful."

Frequent visitors came, many of them bringing food. Lois had been active in scouting, active in the school her children attended, and had been a volunteer at the Notre Dame Health Center. Friends and teachers came to call and to help. "It always lifted Mom's spirits and our spirits too," Kathy said.

Jack has a sister who lives close and she helped a lot, too. "She still helps," Jack said. He said they had to let a lot of work go and they are still behind, but at the time a lot of things became much less important.

When Jack said he would do it over again, the same way, he added, "and maybe sooner." Kathy feels that maybe the hospice approach isn't for everyone, but she would highly recommend it. Their cost came to about $600. They said they wish more insurance companies would cover this kind of care, a month of which compares in cost to one or two days in a hospital.

Betty's Story

"She was exceptionally strong, mentally, morally and physically." When she realized her battle with cancer was soon to be lost, "she made up her mind she wanted to die at home."

John DiTrapani is talking about his wife, Betty. Married for 22 years, John and Betty had known a very special relationship. "One of two things occur in a marriage with no children," John explained. "Either you discover how great your differences are and end the relationship or you discover and develop something very unique."

In May 1977 Betty had surgery for the removal of a tumor in her abdomen. Even though there was talk of malignancy, she was free of symptoms for almost all of the next two years. "We thought we had it licked," John said.

Betty had worked for 10 years for the county welfare department. In the two years after the surgery, she did part-time work and she and Jack spent time doing one of their favorite things, travelling.

In April 1979 a second operation was necessary. Betty realized at this time that there was more cancer but decided to tell no one, not even her husband.

"She told the doctor she would have him drawn and quartered if he told," John said. "I had had a heart attack in the past and I guess she thought the news might sap me."

She wanted to go to California to visit relatives, so they made the trip in May. She also wanted to see two other doctors there to get their opinions about the kind of chemotherapy she was getting. They happened to be using different drugs out there, so the information Betty got turned out to be more disconcerting than helpful.
In the fall Betty had a colostomy done, which was to be followed by intravenous chemotherapy. John saw in his wife "what a person has to do to steel themselves for this type of treatment procedure." Leaving the hospital seeing her so weak and sick at these times was very painful for John.

On January 6, 1980, Betty was at home sitting in front of the mirror. She had lost all her hair as a result of the chemotherapy. Looking at herself the tears began to stream down her cheeks. It was then that she told John she had about two months to live.

Three days later, when she had her last chemotherapy treatment, one of the nurses who had been working with Betty gave them a pamphlet about the Milwaukee Hospice. Because of Betty's desire to stay at home, they called hospice and someone came out to talk with them that same day.

"The hospice comes to do an interview first," John said, "to determine the wishes of the family unit and to help them decide if they can handle it." For John his personal decision was whether he could personally make it better for her final days. John felt his wife could have handled it by herself but "I don't know if I could have. I needed their psychological support."

Betty wanted to use her time to write notes to her friends. She wanted to plan her own funeral. "I guess you would say my wife and I were not religiously oriented. We did not attend any particular church regularly. So we were not looking for religious sustenance but rather a humanistic approach, human support. Our belief centers around a person or persons taking the responsibility to make it on their own."

They found this kind of support from the professional staff at the hospice. It is not affiliated with any particular religious denomination, but will arrange assistance from a priest, rabbi, or minister for those who wish it. The chaplain-director, James M. Ewens, is a Catholic priest.

"We had such a rapport with the hospice people," John said. "We could talk about death and dying, about anything. I don't know if it happens that way with anyone else, but for us it was special rapport."

In the weeks that followed, John and Betty reached a deeper level of sharing. "After 22 years of marriage we were really in tune," John said, "about life in general and the things we enjoyed like music and travel."

John believes, "Everybody has a private part of themselves, but we were able to share that too during those last two months." Betty wanted to take less than the prescribed amount of pain medication so she could use her opportunities to talk with John and her family and friends.

Even when Betty became more wasted physically, she enjoyed the visits of friends. "The initial conversation might be hesitant," John said, "but she would put them at ease. Everyone who left the house went away uplifted. They only left when they saw she was tiring."

John and Betty's relatives, two brothers and a sister, were very helpful too. He has worked at Allis Chalmers for 25 years, presently with sales and advertising, and they were very understanding about his taking extra days off from work to be at home. When he had to go in for a day or two a week her family would come to be with her.

After Betty had had her last treatment, John felt she rejected her body, considering it only a vehicle for her spirit, the essence of her being. He was convinced of this when a hospice nurse offered her a remedy for her dry skin and she refused it.

John praised the hospice staff for their help and support. "They are strong and marvelous and most helpful," he said, "and they are just as interested in the survivors."

The night before Betty died she refused her pain medication even though she was quite uncomfortable. John called the hospice for advice. He was told that when someone is that low he should have been making the decision for her. It made him think of Betty's unselfishness. "I realized Betty would not want me to be complaining to anyone else about her lot."

Betty died the next morning. Kathie Harrison was there the entire day, "providing an additional arm, additional strength," he said.

In March, on the anniversary of Betty's death, John wrote a letter. He said, "There may have been some corny lines in there but I talked about the importance of family surroundings: the homestead, Grandma's afghan, the old bedstead. I may have been conceived on that bedstead myself."

He said at home you are not as far as a buzzer away. You can always be there. Every time you leave the hospital the departure becomes more dramatic. "Even when someone has gotten so weak there are some really good moments. You don't want to miss them," he said. She never lost her sense of humor and he treasures that memory too.

"I feel for myself everything was done," John said. "No twinges, no guilt." He feels it has helped his own healing too.

"She was a remarkable person," he said. "I still have difficulty talking about her with the people who knew her. When sharing memories, the tears come out, but they're coming less often now. Betty told me, 'There'll be a time, for a long time, when you'll think about me and cry. And then there'll be a time when you'll think about me and smile.'"

John's Story

It was just a year ago that he finally decided to do something about that growth on his shoulder. Being an accountant, the last few months had been busy for him, as they always were.

But last May his wife, Fran, insisted once again, "Tax time is over now. It's time to do something about it." And she was surprised that John agreed at last and said, "You're right."

So John Schmittner went in to the hospital as an out-patient to have the growth on his shoulder removed. The next day they called to tell him it was a melanoma, or malignant tumor. They wanted him to come in to the hospital on Monday for more tests to determine how much of his body was affected.

Fran expected John to be in the hospital about a week. But when she went to visit and bring him some things on Tuesday, she found her husband standing in front of the hospital with his suitcase. He got in the car and said, "Just go home. It's all over but the shouting."

The first tests John had done that morning had already proven that the cancer had invaded his entire system. For this Wauwatosa family the shock of John's diagnosis would soon be affecting six children as well as John and Fran.

"He was a big man," Fran said, "and he was always healthy. He was never ill; he never even had colds." But looking back she thought that in the past months there had been some subtle changes in addition to the shoulder tumor which had started out like a tiny mole.

Fran said the diagnosis was a very big blow, but in a very short time John set the tone for how they were to deal with it. "He was angry for a few minutes," she said, "and I do mean minutes. Then there were tears for a few minutes."

But after that he announced, "Now let's get things done."

In the days that followed John proceeded to call all the people he did accounting or tax work for, telling of his situation so they would have time to look for someone to replace him. "They were so surprised," Fran said, "that he could be thinking of others at a time like that."

Because he was so strong, she could be too, Fran said. In the beginning she was thinking that cancer is a word everyone is frightened of, but maybe it's not the worst.

They decided to see another doctor. The first doctor did not suggest any treatment and told John he probably had about six months or less to live. The second doctor said they could try chemotherapy treatments, even though they are not effective in most cases like John's. But he told them, "You can never know when it might turn things around."

John had a bad seizure on June 21. Fran said she called an ambulance and he was taken to Milwaukee County Hospital. They wanted to do a CAT scan but since it was a Saturday, the weekend went by and the test hadn't been done. Monday John decided to leave the hospital, but he did consent to the test a few days later. The test showed the disease had travelled to his brain.

Radiation treatments were prescribed to try to minimize pain, so Fran took him several times a week for chemotherapy and radiation.

It was near the end of June, during one of the treatment sessions, that the doctor talked to Fran about Milwaukee Hospice. "That was the day I really knew how bad he was," Fran said. "Before that I guess it still hadn't registered."

On July 15, Fran and John were at the table doing paperwork for about two hours. John was very alert but was having trouble, dropping papers frequently, which Fran was not paying too much attention to. But a short time later he suffered a stroke and was again taken to the hospital.

The stroke caused paralysis of his left side and his speech was somewhat slurred, but he was alert. He stayed in the hospital about two weeks to finish the radiation treatments.

The decision to use Milwaukee Hospice services came almost by instinct, Fran said. "John did not like hospitals at all. He was eager to know he could be at home."

She thought it would be easier to take care of him in the den but found it hard to bring up the idea. She felt it might make it more difficult for someone who had always been so independent to realize that now he needed help. "Put me wherever you want," John said, "as long as you take me home."

Two of the older Schmittner children are married and two others had also left home. Daughter Mary, 22, had been working with a children's theater group in Providence, R.I., and could have continued in that work. But before her father became ill she had decided to come home for the summer and get a job here.

"Why do these things happen?" Fran asked. It was Mary's help that made it all manageable for Fran. And Mary took her youngest sister, Liz, 8, with her during the day to her job with the Brown Deer Recreation Department. A son, John, 21, who had been away, also happened to return home about this time.

The day John came home from the hospital, a hospice nurse came to help set things up. She came every other day for a while to see how things were going and to answer questions.

"No way could we have handled it without them," Fran said. "The nights are the longest and you can call them any time. And they reassure you that you are doing the right thing."

She had special praise for Mary New, director of volunteers, a vital part of the hospice support system. "One night I was just so shook for no special reason. I called Mary about 1] p.m. and she came right over. We just talked. I don't think a friend or neighbor would have been the same. And they're super with the kids, too, talking with them."

Those were busy weeks. Fran said, "There was no time to think or worry." Family life went on. Liz and Joe, 13, liked to sit and talk with Dad. Since John enjoyed smoking, they sat with him when he had a cigarette in case he dozed off.

"From day one the kids were part of every discussion," Fran said. "We told the truth. We were very open. During that time I was so busy I don't think I worried that much about how they were doing or how they would accept it."

She did have a one-to-one chat with each child to see how they were doing, she said. She told them it was up to God. She told them to pray for Dad, but whatever God decided was what they had to accept. She thinks their honest and matter-of-fact approach helped the children.

Their questions took different shapes. Young Liz wondered what she would do if something happened to Mom. But she answered her own question. "I know: I'll call Teresa (her married sister) and she'll come and get me." One of the boys was worried about where the money would come from if Dad didn't work.

Fran definitely feels at peace about the way John's care was handled. "It was the best way we could have gone," she said. "It allowed us to function much more continually as a family. The other family members could have the most time with him this way."

John preferred that Fran was nearby. Whenever she needed to leave to do something, he greeted her with, "Boy, you sure were gone a long time," even when the "long time" was only a few minutes.

"There are times you wonder if you are going to last," she said, "when you are so tired you can't function. But when it's over it seems like such a short time." John lived only one month more.

"I don't know if we could have done it if we were in our seventies. I do know I couldn't have done it without the kids."

Daughter Mary, who played such a key role in her father's care, has written down some of her thoughts. Even though she had doubts at first that the home care plan would work, she said, "I have changed a great deal since I've experienced my father's death. I feel that I understand life better than I ever have. I think the best thing that happened during the time before my father died was the fact that we could have him at home with the entire family. A lot of people ask 'Why did you take care of your father at home?' and the answer is 'Love.'"

When Mary went back to Providence in October she wrote the following poem and sent it to her mother.

Life can be long,
Or Life can be short,
Dying is quick,
Or dying is slow,
What does it mean?
And where do we go?
Oh please, God:
Help me to grow.

Some things are white
And some things are black,
Why is this death thing
Neither of that?
Open the door,
Just a crack,
Let me see,
Oh please let me grow.

Some days the door
Seems open a crack
But don't look back
'Cause its lock is on tight.
Someday the Answer will come
When you're all alone
And you're out the door
Until that Day,
Oh God, dear God,
Help me to grow,
Help me to grow.

Kay's Story

Kay Boemer is the center of a busy household. Involvement with people who need her is what keeps her busy, people like her husband and six active school-age children.

But a year ago she was faced with a different challenge. Her father needed her, too. Kay brought him from Detroit to their home to care for him during his final illness.

Marshall Bruce, Kay's 68-year-old father, loved life and loved people. Kay called him a "very positive, outgoing and trusting person." It was important to him to be involved in as much of life as he could be.

Eleven years earlier, when he was 57, he had undergone surgery for the removal of a rectal cancer. According to Kay, he was extremely ill at that time and they did not know if he would live.

Marshall not only recovered but also returned to a full life and full schedule, managing his own business and working as a semi-professional singer. In addition to these activities he became active in local and national Ostomy Societies, self-help and support groups for persons who had experienced surgery similar to his own.

Things went well and Marshall stayed healthy for nine years. Then a recurrent tumor made it necessary to have a lung removed. For the next two years the disease spread to other parts of his body. It affected his other lung and the condition was inoperable. Then there was evidence of a bone tumor.

"He was still leading a full life," said Kay. He was getting radiation treatments and experimental chemotherapy. "And I think sheer willpower kept him going."

When he could fight it no longer and entered the hospital last spring, Kay went to Detroit to see about his care. What she hoped to do was to set up 24-hour nursing care for him in his own home. While she did find nurses were available, she realized that she could not coordinate this kind of arrangement without being on the scene.

In subsequent discussions with her father and three brothers, none of whom lived in the Detroit area, it was decided that her father could either be cared for in a nursing home or come to Brookfield to live with Kay's family.

Marshall decided to come there and Kay's husband and family agreed it was a good decision. "There are so few things in life that you feel sure are really right, but as soon as we had him here we knew this was right for all of us," Kay said.

There were challenges to be worked out on many fronts. "We were able to get the use of a hospital bed and bedside stand free from the local American Cancer Society," Kay said. He needed to be transported by wheelchair to County General Hospital for radiation to relieve pain. A neighbor boy sometimes helped Kay with that.

"It was delightful having him home," said Kay, even though watching his decline was like "letting air out of a balloon." While he could face the reality of dying, he felt angry at first, she said, and was repelled at the thought of being sick.

Here is one of the ways support from Milwaukee Hospice Inc. helped the family work through some of these thoughts and feelings. "I can't imagine doing it without them," said Kay. "They take you where you are and offer you a perspective."

Her father was experiencing a grieving process for himself, the reality of the loss of his singing, his job, and his children, she said.

Hospice personnel helped in other ways. Although Kay had not had previous nursing experience, she was not frightened at the prospect of caring for her father. But she was concerned and wanted him to have the best possible care.

"They gave me practical instruction to give me the expertise I needed," Kay said. She learned how to move and bathe him, manage his nutrition and his pain medication.

"Professionals are available 24 hours a day for consultation about changes that occur, the times you just get the feeling that something is wrong or something is different," she said. They will have someone come and check or expedite phone calls to the physician for changes in medication.

The course of her father's illness began to naturally involve the family in his care. The children helped to move him and understood it was important to be careful and gentle.

One of the daughters like to massage Grandpa's feet when poor circulation added to his discomfort. She just seemed to be naturally good at this and enjoyed doing it. They colored pictures for him and shared stories. He taught them all his mind-twister games, and they did puzzles and watched TV together.

"He dearly loved children and people," Kay said, "and there was real stimulation value in his being at home."

As multiple tumors in his brain developed, it affected his thinking some of the time. There would be periods when he was semi-comatose and then moments of recognition. One day while Kay was standing at the bedside, she didn't think her father was aware that she was telling her children which jobs to do to get the house straightened up.

When daughter Lucy came with the sisterly complaint, "Ginny isn't helping me clean our room," Kay gave the word about how Ginny and should help. Lucy proceeded to bellow out the command.

Grandpa opened his eyes and observed, "That Lucy certainly can communicate," and then slipped back to not responding again. And Kay remembered, "I'd be changing the bed and he'd reach up and pull me down toward him."

At these times Kay knew how special it can be for a child to fulfill these needs for a parent, a parent who always gave and never asked for anything for himself, and she was grateful to be available all the time, which is not possible in the hospital.

Kay also experienced a new level of sharing with her three brothers during her father's final illness. "It made me realize what neat men they really are," she said. She always felt close to them even though they now lived too far apart to see much of each other.

"Whenever I needed a break, one of them would be here," she said. She felt a deepened trust and knowledge that they would indeed "always be there for each other."

Kay had her father in a small room close to the kitchen at first to give him some privacy. "But when we knew he was dying, we moved his bed into the family room," she said. The family routine went on and even the children's friends shared the matter-of-fact awareness of Grandpa's illness.

"My Grandpa got sick and came here to die," one of the children said. And whenever Grandpa could, he had a handshake and greeting for whomever came by.

As the children witnessed his increasing pain it helped prepare them for his death. Even though they were very sad, they could see, "His body was too tired to live anymore," or "It is good that he won't have to groan anymore."

Kay said, "There is a feeling of relief when someone is free of pain. When you see the body can handle no more, you are grateful." The Milwaukee Hospice was helpful at this time too. "After my dad died in July," said Kay, "they were interested in us for us." They help families work through the grieving process.

When a friend of Kay's came to express her sympathy, she said, "I wonder if you know how blessed you are. Most of us have parents who teach us how to live. But your father also taught you how to die." Kay said, "He thought enough of us and trusted us enough to share his dying with us."

A Nurse's Story

"I never thought I could do all that I did...." This statement is made many times by family members who take care of a patient at home. The goal of the hospice nurse in this setting is not to take over the responsibility for the patient's care; rather, it is to assist the family in providing this care themselves. This includes teaching the family caretakers, being available for emergencies, and helping prepare the family for what might happen next.

Another part of the nurse's role has to do with facilitating lines of communication. Sometimes patients become confused and say things that they are not fully aware of or responsible for. Family members need to understand why this happens, and to interpret the symptoms, words, and actions of the patient. Nurses help to keep physicians alert to changes in a patient's condition, thereby ensuring that appropriate medication is available for pain control. They also inform families of resources available from community agencies such as the American Cancer Society, in-patient hospital units, and companies that will deliver equipment and medications to a patient's home.

During these first two years of caring for dying patients two things have stood out for me: 1. All the roles change when a patient's care occurs at home. Family members provide the primary care, while nurses and physicians assume more supportive, subsidiary roles. Necessary decisions are made with full participation by the patient, the family, and health care professionals. 2. The environment of loving care that permeates the home setting is as important as any specialized nursing skill I can bring to a patient. Families know instinctively what foods are most likely to be appreciated, who should be allowed private visiting time, and when a patient's condition has changed. The professional health care person coming into the home must be attuned to the suggestions given by the patient and family so that nothing is omitted or ignored in the physical and psychosocial care.

Alice Prochniewski, R.N.

A Doctor's Story

The word "cancer" evokes many images for people, but perhaps the most significant one is fear: fear of being abandoned, fear of death and the unknown, fear of pain. This latter fear is a real part of many cancer problems. Its control is essential if a cancer patient is to experience an optimal quality of life. And pain can be controlled in 85% of the patients with cancer.

Three aspects are important:

A. Adequate types of medication to handle the pain;
B. Delivery of the medication at appropriate intervals;

C. Supportive caregivers who can work with the apprehensions associated with the pain problem.

Too often pain medication is given PRN (as often as is necessary). This inevitably leaves a period of time between a patient's awareness of returning pain and the time required for additional medication to be administered and have its proper effect. For terminally ill patients one could generally say, "Never give medication PRN." Instead, pain medication should be given on a regular schedule—every three or four hours—with the dose adjusted to handle the entire time interval. This enables a patient's system to create a reservoir of pain resistance. It also reduces apprehensions about the pain returning. Properly given, pain medication is not habit-forming; in fact, with careful attention to appropriate dosage and time intervals, many patients are able to reduce the overall amount of medication they need for their pain to be controlled.

John Hurley, M.D.

A Chaplain's Story

When I look back on the people and experiences of the past two years as a hospice staff member, a collage of images and words comes to mind. I think of the response given by a man who was asked what he found helpful from those who came to visit him: "The chance to be myself—hopeful, angry, whatever—and still be listened to and appreciated."

I am impressed with the sense of gratitude shown by a couple who were a few years short of their golden wedding anniversary, but who celebrated it early because they wanted to thank their family and friends for all they had shared in and received.

There is delight in remembering the tiny, frail woman in her seventies who began crying when I asked how she was feeling. To comfort her I reached out and briefly held her hand. When her daughter returned to the room and noticed the tears she asked why she was crying. Her mother responded in Spanish, and the two of them broke out in laughter. I asked what the mother had said and the daughter replied, "She said that you pinched her."

Equal amounts of wonder and mystery shine through in the life of Jeff Dallman, a 30-year-old diabetic who experienced dialysis, the temporary loss of his eyesight, a bone graft, and a successful kidney transplant, all within 18 months' time. Then, a year later, he and his wife heard the happy news that she was pregnant with their first child.

There is a feeling of achievement in the words a daughter wrote after the death of her mother: "At the time of need hospice gave us hope. It helped us to focus on the essential tasks, and to let the rest take care of itself."

The ups and downs of coping with loss are evident in these two statements made by widows: "Sorrow, anger, lack of crying, wondering if you can manage to keep on living—these are normal, expected reactions to the loss of a loved one." "Being a widow may be a new phase of growth for me, but it is certainly not one of my favorite phases."

I mention all of these because they suggest the full range of emotions and struggles that our families contend with, both during the time of illness and in the bereavement period that follows. A major goal of hospice is to free the family to be together, rather than their being wearied with burdens beyond their strength. This is achieved by both the professional expertise each staff member has and the personal attention given to the unique needs of each family.

The briefest, best definition of hospice that I know says that hospice is the fullness of life. This can only occur because of the spirit of courage shown by families and the trust that they place in the health care professionals who enter their lives at a critical juncture.

James Ewens

CHAPTER THREE

Reflections on the Hospice Experience

Editor's Note: Hospice staff members assist families in caring for a dying person at home. A short while after the person has died the staff writes a letter to the family, asking them to evaluate the care that was given, how they felt about the wake and funeral, and any other things that helped or hurt them during this time. Here are the suggestions that came in as a response to this request, along with some of the reflections they composed after the patient's death had occurred.

* * * * *

Tell people to visit even if the patient cannot talk; sitting and holding a person's hand is very comforting. Transfer things into the spouse's name sometime before the death—it makes things a lot simpler afterwards in terms of financial arrangements. Visit as much as possible. Respect the wishes of the person regarding the choice of treatment. The more you can share with the spouse in those final months, the better. And remember to call on the bereaved after the first month.

* * * * *

I was very fortunate to have the cooperation from my husband after we learned he had cancer. He was aware that his time was limited and we talked everything over each step of the way. We had our attorney come to the house and he helped my husband make out a will. He also advised me to begin a personal bank account so I drew out quite a bit of money from our joint account and started a savings account in my name. My husband's insurance policies were all in good order. He had the beneficiaries named on each policy. It is heart-breaking to talk about wills and insurance policies, but I think it is very important to do so while the sick person is still capable of talking and thinking for himself.

The funeral director also was most cooperative. He took care of the church services, the cemetery arrangements, gave me suggestions on ordering funeral flowers and explained that it really was not necessary to buy the most expensive casket.

We had bought a crypt a few years ago when he retired which also helped. After the funeral I had people to a restaurant for a brunch which seemed to be a good way for us to talk and wind down together. Since that time I have tried to keep myself busy and get involved in new groups. Three months after his death I joined a senior citizens' group. We meet every Thursday. We take trips, have socials, see movies together, and play cards. Whenever anybody asks me to go to some affair I never say no. These all help, but I still miss my husband a lot and have a good cry now and then when I'm by myself. The days are busy but the nights are still lonesome.

* * * * *

One thing I regret is that the death notice was not better written. We were rushed for time and things were omitted that I think would have made more people aware of my husband's death and all that he was involved in during his life.

What did help was that the lawyer was familiar with the family and had taken care of their business for many years. As I now go to sell some stocks and bonds, I find this is a very complicated and time-consuming procedure, but there isn't anything that can be done about that.

* * * * *

What was helpful during the bereavement period: most helpful was time. I was alone for several days while my family went skiing the week after the funeral. I hardly left the house, saw and talked to very few people. Mostly just stayed home, tried to straighten up things, allowed myself to cry as much and as often as I felt like it. Then a few weeks later I was alone again for five days—and I did more of the same.

* * * * *

The understanding and sympathy of friends was intensely appreciated. The day we came back from the funeral in Illinois one of my friends made a complete meal for my family and left in on the front porch. I will never forget the intense feeling of love I had for this heart that I knew was touching mine.

* * * * *

The hospice nurse stayed in the house with us for several hours after mother died at home, even though it was 5 a.m. and she was getting ready to leave town that morning for her Christmas vacation. This gave us a chance to think things over, ask whatever questions we had about the death and the burial, etc. It was so helpful in a practical way—and also gave me a feeling of total support, as if there were some foundation under me, as if whatever I needed, she would help with.

I can't begin to reiterate the aggravation of a doctor not knowing what was wrong, not telling us, not helping to alleviate her pain. Her medical care was a horror. She constantly complained of a pain high in her chest which no doctor ever diagnosed, though I think that is what she eventually died of. One doctor gave her an EKG and said, "She's okay; her heart's all right." None ever suggested a chest x-ray. Another doctor later guessed, "Well, maybe it's gone into her lungs." They gave her medication which affected her in all kinds of terrible ways (constipation, etc.) without regard for the side effects. They didn't want to take the time, they didn't want to be bothered, they were inhumane—I can't say enough bad words about them.

Two weeks before she died her doctor said, "Oh yes, the chemotherapy is working so well, she can plan to travel to Boston." Then, when she was weakened by an intense bout of constipation, he gave her a dose of chemo that ripped her veins going in and from which she never recovered, and she died ten days later. I realize she was going to die anyway, and maybe sooner was better, but somehow it was so stupidly done that it was very painful to us.

The nurses in the hospital, especially on weekends, were not very present. We finally found one nurse we could confer with. She was the only one who told us what was wrong; she was compassionate and honest and seemed to care if the right drugs were prescribed or if any were, etc., etc.

One final thing. Although my mother's condition was terminal, we tried the chemotherapy. This was probably a mistake physically and emotionally, for it caused her more pain than it alleviated. Yet psychologically we need to feel we were trying everything. We had had no experience with cancer, had no idea what taking that treatment was going to be like. You could have helped us then by telling us just what the results would be and pointing out that it probably was not the best way. Also, by accepting her as a patient even though she was still receiving chemo.

Lord, why do you do the things you do?
I love you, Lord, so where's my reward?
I know I don't deserve one, but sometimes it's hard to
love you, Lord, for what you do.

You take people away and you don't return them the
next day.
Oh, Lord, if you love us, why do you make us cry?
We sin automatically, not purposely.
We don't mean to hurt you, so Lord,
Why do you do the things you do?

Stacy Young, age 11½

* * * * *

If I were to describe in one word my feelings about the
help I received when my husband was dying, it would be
"security." When you are caring for a loved one in their
final days it is likely to be a first experience for you.
To have someone who is capable and caring available to
you 24 hours a day, seven days a week—this is a security
blanket without equal at such a time.

Many things were included as part of this security
umbrella for me: skilled nursing available on short
notice, pain control for my husband, teaching help for
me so I could be ready for new demands as they arose.
Then too, I appreciated the concern for myself—how I
was holding up, what kinds of breaks I needed along the
way. Another relief was not having to deal with
insurance companies and other suppliers of needs.
Fortunately for me, many volunteers were available to
us from our church, but I know the hospice would have
provided them for the asking.

Finally, I wish to comment on the bereavement follow-
up. What a comfort to have a continuing relationship

with the hospice staff as you face the first months in your new world. Their visits helped me deal with the various broken parts of my life, in a way that friends could not. I'm grateful to have received the under-standing and supportive help I needed during this past year of change.

* * * * *

I found out I had lung cancer in November]979. I tried to deal with this, and then learned in March]980 that it had spread to the brain. The doctor at West Allis Memorial gave me six to eight months to live. Since then my own friends and the hospice staff have been a source of strength for me. I'm amazed at the way people have responded to my own need for caring these days: neighbors, my bosses at West Allis Memorial, people who were unknown to me until a few months back.

It's a funny thing. In this mixed-up world we feel that people are too busy to help out—and then we find out that everyone cares, really cares. That's even happened between myself and God. I shout at him sometimes and ask for help. I guess we all get closer to him when we are in need. My son and daughter are in this with me too—together we shall manage to accept it and work it through to the end.

I've done what I can—my bills are paid, I have a roof over my head, and there's a peace of mind now. The struggle is not to let it get you down in the day-by-day. I'm learning to ask others for help. At times this is very hard, with lots of good and bad days along the way. With the help of old and new-found friends I'll make it until the Lord calls me.

* * * * *

Even though I have lost my husband Gary, and the tears slide down my face so rapidly, Thanksgiving returns. My loss is overwhelming, yet my thankfulness becomes more intense with each new day. The season of Thanksgiving has not changed, but its meaning has.

In comparison to other years, my husband and I were blessed abundantly during his final year of life. On July]5th Gary was not expected to live more than twenty-four hours, but he lived another seven weeks past that time. And because of the help we received from a local hospice group, Gary and I were able to share precious moments together in the privacy of our own home.

The magnitude of the love exchanged between us and all who entered our home must have caused God to smile. The true essence of life was never more clear to us, and the genuine love of God could be seen in the courage and strength my husband expressed at this time. He taught all of us to keep on the positive side of life, and to find a way around any obstacle.

As I continue to move forward in the aftermath of this unique experience I will remain thankful that the Lord still gives me the will to live and the insight to appreciate his care for me. Gary's words still ring in my ears, "Tell everyone who helped me that I love them—and thanks for everything."

* * * * *

Dear Mom and Dad,

This is just a note to let you know that you're in our constant thoughts and prayers. I'm out of advice, I'm out of cliches; I'm very frustrated and confused by these past long difficult months—but somehow, I'm not out of hope. The hopes that some peace and some understanding will come out of all this, whenever God reveals Himself to us.

I've learned a lot about coping and overcoming from you two, and from Lea and the rest of the relatives.   I'm glad I can pass this heritage of strength along to the girls. They too will face unbearably hard times— everyone does—but at least they'll know that it can be done.

Please remember, Dad, that it is <u>your</u> body and you have a right to every decision about it. If you've had enough, you've had enough. If you want to keep fighting, fight.

You do not belong to the hospital, to the doctors, to research, or even to us—only to yourself and God and what you decide together. We love you both and want the very highest quality of life for you.

God's Blessings and Strength

* * * * *

I ask not for a faith
that will move a mountain,
but for a faith that will
sometimes move me.

Life is eternal and love
is immortal; death is only
a horizon, and horizon is
nothing save the limit of our sight.

* * * * *

I am astounded at the amount of love offered me these days. It is like opening Christmas presents in the middle of summer. Is it that my unexpected vulnerability has made me more receptive of others' concern?   Most of my masks have been torn away by fear. My defenses are pretty damned thin after all. I feel so flayed by the disease and the treatment for it, my spiritual pain and physical weakness are revealed for all to see. Because I have given—or so it seems—my very will over to the medical profession, strangers, I cling to those who offer love.

* * * * *

We've just found out that Jane has pneumonia and that it's just a matter of hours. For her sake I don't want her to have to live this way much longer, but thinking that way makes me feel guilty. Last night, even though I had been warned that she had lost her normal color and a lot of weight, just a peek from the doorway made me jump. But as I looked closer I found that she didn't look so bad. Still, after all this time I've been here, every new time I walk in the door I still have to first just peek, because I know I'll have to get that first shock over with.

I'm sitting next to her now, and as I look up I realize how different she is. The hardest thing is to think that Grandma Jane will never again be the same. This isn't just a momentary thing, not something that in a few days will be over, and there will be Grandma Jane, all shining and new, the same as always. I don't think I'll ever to be able to face the fact that she's going to die. Somehow when you talk about the woman in this bed dying, you're just talking about the woman in this bed dying. Not Grandma Jane. It can't be Grandma Jane. She didn't look like the woman dying in this bed. No, she was strong, healthy, and beautiful—not fragile and struggling to breathe.

I don't think Grandma Jane wanted to die this way. So awful, so prolonged. But I think it's her fighting that has kept her alive. That, and the fact that she knows how much love is all around her. In this hard way a lot of new love has been aroused.

CHAPTER FOUR

Suggested Readings

The Hospice Movement: A Better Way To Care For The Dying by Sandol Stoddard. New York: Random House, 1978.

On Death and Dying by Elisabeth Kubler-Ross. New York: The Macmillan Company, 1969.

A Private Battle by Cornelius Ryan and Kathryn Morgan Ryan. New York: Fawcett-Popular Library, 1979.

The Death of Ivan Ilich by Leo Tolstoy. New York: New American Library, 1960.

Something Beautiful for God by Malcolm Muggeridge. New York: Harper & Row, 1971.

PART III
The Support System

Hospice emphasizes the concept of holistic care. All aspects of the patient-family needs are considered worthy of attention and response. In particular, when decisions are made, health care professionals encourage patients and families to participate fully in both the discussion of options and the final choice made. This enables families and outside professionals to work closely together as peers, so that quality care can be given in all situations. It also brings hospice staff members and families into closer types of relationships than would ordinarily occur in an institutional setting. This chapter presents how these contacts and this work affect the health care professionals involved in it.

CHAPTER FIVE

The Support System:
Who Provide It and How It Can Help

The cumulation of experience in their own lives prepared them for this work as much as or more than their actual professional training. "I knew there must be a better way," the nurses agreed, "and everything in my life prepared me for this experience."

With backgrounds in chaplaincy, nursing, and social work, the hospice staff were not strangers to death and dying. But the roles they were playing as individuals left them with some feelings of inadequacy. By coming to work together they found they were better able to coordinate their philosophies and develop an integrated program that more fully meets the needs of the people they are committed to serve. In the process of caring for the needs of their patients they have also found they form a vital support system for each other.

"Families can learn to do anything out of love." On the basis of this philosophy, the hospice staff helps families believe and accomplish this when faced with a terminal illness. They provide the kind of encouragement to families that enables them to make their own decisions. "We don't have all the answers, but we see that people can heighten their own abilities by deciding to do something rather than having it done for them."

for a family is OK. Their experience in working with families has shown them that they are not there to teach people how to die or how to cope, but rather to provide a support system in which people find their own ways to deal with what is going on around them.

The hospice staff usually sends both a nursing person and a support person to the home, but they find the roles they may find themselves playing can change and overlap, just as they do within the family itself. They rarely know how a pattern will evolve for an individual or a family. And they stay open and sensitive to which of their staff will work most comfortably with a given family.

Even in some of the physical aspects of nursing care they find themselves asking as often as telling how to do things: "Show me how you do that," or "He's more used to your hands than mine." They find that families show a lot of creativity and ability to improvise as well as real competence.

Since support on all levels is so vital, they try to summarize what they do in this concept: "This is tough stuff, but we're in it together. We'll go through it with you."

A staff worker observes, "There aren't a lot of things that surprise me anymore. I know it's OK not to know answers. I know it's OK just to be there. To share that with families is freeing for me. They accept our sense of helplessness and it helps them to accept their own."

In caring for their first 250 families the hospice staff has learned that you can't predict when someone is going to die. They have learned by being on 24-hour call how important it is to be able to sense the urgency in a phone call when there is some kind of change, even when it can be poorly defined or explained. They know when a family needs them.

"And some of our best visits are the leisurely ones. We have the advantage of being not too structured. Sometimes you learn more when one person leaves the room or someone wants to walk you to the car."

The 250 families served represent all different backgrounds, a broad spectrum from the very rich to the very poor and many different religious persuasions. "In a given day or a given week we have to shift gears many times. The diversity has made me much more accepting of people's differences. My whole idea of nursing has done a]80-degree turn. I know I don't have to keep my distance but I can be a friend, accepted by the family. People have said to me, 'I knew you were OK when you came in your jeans and sat on the floor.' "

Another staff members notes, "Hospice is really nothing more than zeroing in on all the needs we always have, mind, body, and soul. But perhaps the best part about it is allowing people to be who they are in the midst of life and death. Dying is a damn hard, very private thing to do. It's seldom beautiful and so difficult to get to with any dignity. My hope is that I can continue to learn, to be sensitive, to be fooled, to be surprised. Because when I think I can call it, or know it all, I will have lost my effectiveness."

In working with families the hospice staff is also sensitive to the needs of children when children are involved. Children can be very direct or reluctant to talk at all about what they are feeling or experiencing. When the physical needs of a dying patient are dominating the scene, hospice personnel are perceptive to the other family needs that are going on at the same time.

They help families realize that other kinds of support are available to them and how to be willing to use them. At times like this friends, neighbors, and other relatives are often glad for the opportunity to bring in meals and do laundry or errands if they are allowed to do so.

In their concern for entire families the hospice staff involves itself with the whole reality of bereavement. Even when people feel the most lost and empty, their lives do go forward. They are comforted by visits from the staff in their homes. Families react with gratitude and surprise because someone is concerned about them. It is sometimes a frustration that they can't spend more time with these kinds of contacts because they feel it is still an area that is poorly understood and that there is a great need for the right support in working through the loss of a loved one.

Professionals involved in this kind of work find they personally have to deal with some of the same fears and pains in themselves that the families they are helping are experiencing.

They consider their work extremely satisfying rather than depressing. The constant exposure to the end of life can bring a deeper appreciation of life and the importance of living it fully. "You are prepared for death if you are prepared for life." They feel too that this kind of work "helps us accept our own humanness" with all its limitations.

As with the families they serve, they are sometimes faced with the awareness of a certain heaviness. "I find occasionally that I don't realize how sad I am. I don't know how it is going to come out, but I hope when it does it will be in some way that is appropriate."

They have fears too when they see what some people have to go through. They sometimes wonder if they have the strength to go through it again, to make another attachment and in a short time face another separation.

"We have to live with our limitations too. We can't expect to be Superwoman." So there are times when it's important to know that as much as you would like to do something, you just can't do it right now. "I can't wash my hands of all that pain in the same day."

They have the respect of other professionals and good working relationships with their patients' doctors. Their best moments are being able to share both highs and lows very fully with families because of the kind of exposure their unique service affords. "And humor is central to the job. It is the leveling agent for patients, for families, and for us. It's good for everybody and it brings back perspective. And it helps people know that they will laugh again."

CHAPTER SIX

The Hospice Nurse

I thought it would be easy to write about what I have learned the past two years as a hospice nurse. But as I search to find the words to express my feelings I realize how hard it is. How can I best describe that which is most personal and meaningful to me? My work these years has forced me to redefine what counts most and how I want to live my life now.

My work gives me satisfaction, and the families I meet give me hope and courage. There is something special about being accepted into someone's home during a time of crisis. And it is healing to continue to see family members after a death. The families I have dealt with show me it is all right not to have all the answers. And I have learned that the most helpful things are sometimes accomplished by being present, accepting what is, and listening as fully as I can.

My own family and friends have become more important to me. These are the people I turn to for help, affection, and love. I am closer to my two sisters and my mother since I began this job. I have learned not to wait to tell them how I feel, be it happy, angry, sad, or carefree. We are more open with each other and share ourselves more fully. This is a fringe benefit that comes from my daily work experiences. I realize more and more that time runs out for all of us, and I do not want to be caught short. But I realize I will be caught short on some things. I am working on accepting this, and on being afraid to reveal too much of myself. As I accept the part of me that holds back, so too do my friends and family.

Another thing I have learned is the miracle of laughter. Humor has gotten me through more than one delicate situation. I am now more able to laugh at myself and not take things so seriously. It not only relieves tension, but I believe it also eases pain and sorrow.

What this all comes down to is that I have gotten back to the basics, and that means people with whom I can share myself, with tears, love, and laughter.

Kathie Harrison, R.N.

CHAPTER SEVEN

Suggested Readings

Images of Hope by William F. Lynch. New York: The New American Library, 1965.

Aging: The Fulfillment of Life by Henri Nouwen and Walter Gaffney. Garden City, New York: Doubleday, 1976.

Royal Victoria Hospital Manual On Palliative Hospice Care by Ina Ajemian and Balfour Mount. New York: Arno Press, 1980.

A Hospice Handbook by Michael Hamilton and Helen Reid. Erdmans Publishing Company, 1980

PART IV
Children and Hospice

I drew the way my father looked at a bird lying on its side against the curb near our house. "Is it dead, Papa?" I was six, and could not bring myself to look at it.
"Yes," I heard him say in a sad and distant way.
"Why did it die?"
"Everything that lives must die."
"Everything?"
"Yes."
"You too, Papa? And Mama? And me?"
"Yes," he said, and then he added in Yiddish, "but may it be only after you have lived a long and good life, my Asher."
I could not grasp it. I forced myself to look at the bird.
"Why?" I asked.
"That's the way the Ribbono Shel Olom made His world, Asher."
"Why?"
"So life would be precious, Asher. Something that is yours forever is never precious."

From *My Name is Asher Lev* by Chaim Potok. Reprinted with permission. Alfred A. Knopf, Inc., New York, 1972.

It is difficult enough for adults to understand and cope with their own feelings about death. Trying to be of assistance to children at this time is even more challenging. This section will describe how children of different ages think about and respond to the death of a family member.

Chapter Nine is an interview among Phil Donahue, Joy Ufema, R.N., and several women who cared for their children during the final months of life.

Chapter Ten is an account by a woman in Minnesota, Ida Martinson, who has helped over 100 families do the primary care for a dying child in the home context.

CHAPTER EIGHT

Helping Children to
React to Death

Children react to death in many different ways, just as do adults. While we all acknowledge that death is a part of life, the stating of this fact sounds over-simplistic in light of the bewilderment and pain that are associated with the loss of a loved one.

Since a child has not lived long enough to have had the same variety of experiences that adults have known, his or her sense of confusion about death can be more intense. Added to this oftentimes is children's inability to express what they are feeling; their lack of experiences leaves them devoid of even the words to tell what is going on inside them.

When parents try to help their children understand about death, honesty is important. If someone is very ill, sharing the honesty of this fact can be a beginning. "Sometimes doctors can't make people well" is a truth that a child may not yet have experienced.

Many times parents feel that their instincts tell them to protect their children from the realities of death and grief. But this can leave a child feeling more alone and withdrawn than when death is dealt with more openly.

One area children under six or eight have no experience in dealing with is permanence. Death means a person is not going to return, and since a child's orientation is more associated with someone going on a trip, it will take time for him to realize the person won't be here anymore.

One mother related that it took multiple visits to grandpa's house and seeing that grandpa wasn't there before her child began to comprehend that he was indeed gone for good.

Loss of a pet is one experience children may have had that helps them begin to understand the finality of death. Besides introducing a child to permanence, it also teaches him that the sadness and hurt he feels do not last forever. A child learns more from the loss of a pet if it is not immediately replaced.

Knowing that pets die and that plants die in winter help a child to know that this is the way nature works. But it is much harder for him to understand why people die, especially someone he loves.

Caring adults can help children understand that the death of a loved one can make him feel sad, or afraid and even angry. They can help him to realize that understanding this part of life can help him feel better.

One difficulty parents sometimes have is accepting where they are. Their attention span is shorter, for one thing, and the adult tendency to dwell on the loss and over-analyze is usually not necessary for children, especially young children. Answers to questions need not be "so heavy."

A parent's honesty about his own feelings helps children too. When a child hears an adult talk about feeling sad or scared it helps him to accept these feelings in himself. It also helps to hear adults say, "We will get through this."

Some of the questions a child may have are wondering if it will happen to him, whether it was his fault, or if he did something bad that caused it to happen.

It is important to help a child realize that death is never a punishment. It is a natural thing. We have been given wonderfully strong bodies that usually last a long time. But use and time eventually wear out important parts of our bodies and they stop working. Sometimes sickness makes them stop working before a person becomes old. Death is not contagious, and the death of one person does not mean another loved one may also soon die.

Many a child in anger or frustration has felt or said aloud that he wished, perhaps, a parent who was disciplining him were dead or would go away and never come back. This is why he may need reassurance that almost everyone has had thoughts like this from time to time and that in no way does this relate to death.

When a child resumes normal play and laughter it does not mean he is without feeling. He may express denial such as, "My daddy didn't really die." He may express anger, "How could Mom die and leave me all alone?" or, "Why did God let my friend die?"

Sleep is not a good word to use in explaining death. When someone dies, their body stops working. It is not rest. Its job is over.

When someone is terminally ill, it is good to use this time to help the child prepare gradually for death. He will certainly sense, "I don't like what is going on here," and needs explanations and honesty.

Involving a child in the care of a parent or grandparent can help, if the child wants to do this. If he prefers not to be directly involved, he can make contributions in other ways, such as doing errands or helping with other necessary tasks. This can alleviate some of the helplessness or even anger he is experiencing because his life is so disrupted right now.

A child is helped to know that crying is normal and

helpful when he sees adults that he loves cry. When certain events or circumstances cause a parent to burst into tears and a child joins him in weeping, a beneficial sense of mutual support can be established.

The most devastating loss to a child of course is the death of a parent. In the surviving parent's concern for the child, there may be what counselors call "overkill," over-concern or over-compensation, at first. This is all right and may be satisfying some of the parent's own needs at that time.

Maintaining order, stability, and security in the child's life will help the child. Providing warmth, affection, and physical presence will help too. It is not uncommon for a child to express concern, fear, or even panic the first time the surviving parent needs to leave him. It may also take a while before the child is willing to leave and go about his own pursuits.

Sometimes this all goes much more quickly for children than adults, and adults can find themselves resenting the fact that a child seems to be back to business as usual when the adult is having a hard time functioning.

For the young child one reason that this happens, for instance in the loss of a father, is that a lot of the routine of his daily life has not changed that much, since his mother is with him.

School-age children may be afraid to go back to school. They never have told anyone that their parent was sick. They may feel that somehow their loss has made them very different from their peers and, "Would anybody like me anymore?"

Teachers can be helpful to parents when they observe what is going on with the child and keep the parent informed as well as offering their own understanding and reassurance. A child may find himself unable to concentrate, and his grades will suffer. Different personalities react in different ways. A more explosive person may exhibit easily triggered anger over small annoyances. A quiet person who does his crying privately may experience headaches. One five-year-old who lost his father wanted to wear his dad's ties to school because he figured he would have to be the father to his brothers and sisters now.

For the quiet child who doesn't ask anything, a sensitive adult can try subtle ways to help him talk, to let him know he is available for questions or listening. Sometimes when a child realizes his life has changed the questions he has seem too frightening or overwhelming to ask at first.

Very young children may work out some of the reality of their loss through play-acting. "Let's play house. There won't be any daddy in my house because he's dead." Overhearing this may sound harsh to adults, but it is the kind of straightforward simplicity preschoolers may use. Children may also express their feelings when drawing pictures.

They may wonder how holidays are going to change. Will they still be fun? Parents who have lost a partner have sometimes found that it can be helpful to do things a little bit differently or in a different place. If a child has opinions, it is good for him to have input into the plans too.

For teenagers there can be other problems with grief. Since they may have lost their role model, they need to discover with time that, while the person cannot be replaced, he or she may be collectively replaced. When he has the opportunity to relate to other caring adults, such as aunts or uncles, older brothers or sisters, a neighbor or other relatives, the pain of a teenager's loss will begin to diminish.

It is not unusual for a teenager to feel an increased need to develop an intimate relationship with someone of the opposite sex. Heightened sexuality can be very real at this time, as it may also be for the parent, most often the male parent, who has lost his partner.   The great emotional loss unfortunately increases vulnerability. In both cases, when a parent sees this in a child as well as when a child sees it in a parent, it can be threatening and must be dealt with with delicate understanding.

For adolescents, too, the loss of a parent can bring added responsibility. For a] 7-year-old girl who has lost her mother, it may mean planning and preparing meals. Someone has to do the laundry. When the surviving parent is aware that these added responsibilities may be a burden, and does not just take them for granted, it can help alleviate feelings of resentment.

Parents have questions too about wakes and funerals and cemeteries and whether children should participate or be present at these events and if so, at what age.

When a child is first introduced to death, he has a lot of concepts to struggle with. Where did his parents go? Where is heaven? Will he see him again? Why do we put people in the ground?

Depending on his previous experiences, he will certainly have some fears. Some of them may even come from "spooky" stories which at one time were enjoyed. When a grief counselor gave a talk to a group of eighth graders about death, she found that almost every one wanted to be buried above the ground. They also felt that they wouldn't want anyone they love to be cremated because it might hurt.

There is room for a lot of choice when it comes to wakes, funerals, and cemeteries. One pediatrician said that even a child of four can decide for himself if he will attend. If he is told what it will be like and the type of service and that family and friends will be there, he may decide he would like to be there.   He should also be told that people might be sad and possibly cry. Other children may decide they would rather stay home.

If a child does attend a funeral with a sensitive friend who is less intensely grief-stricken, they could also leave easily if the experience became too overwhelming.

A seven-year-old girl refused to believe the death of her sister until she went to the funeral home. The whole custom of viewing the body came into being because of the difficulty in believing someone is dead, so for children as well as adults it can be helpful.

It doesn't have to be all or nothing, either. One parent explained a cemetery as a gentle way to say goodbye to someone we love. She said it was a quiet, pretty place to visit sometimes and bring back good memories.

Most importantly, parents are the best ones to talk with their own children. Others can help support the parent or parents in dealing with this, and reading can be helpful too, but the caring and sensitivity a parent has to offer will help the child the most, and the depth of this kind of sharing will help the parent as well.

Pat Herrington

CHAPTER NINE

The Phil Donahue Show

The following dialogue is excerpted from an interview with Ms. Joy Ufema, Ms. Toni Albert, and Ms. Nancy Staley, December 14, 1979.

Mr. Donahue: You work with all kinds of people as a nurse. You see it all. But you are especially focused on the patient who is dying. I'm fascinated by what you have learned as a result of this experience.

Ms. Ufema: I've learned to set priorities in my life. I learned that we die the way we live. And I learned to go canoeing instead of doing the ironing without feeling guilt for it.

Mr. Donahue: Your point is what—that we have to make time for ourselves?

Ms. Ufema: That's exactly right. And it's because when we're lying on our deathbed, all we have are our memories, and they had better be good ones that feel good for me as a person.

Mr. Donahue: Do you ever tell people they are going to die?

Ms. Ufema: No, not ever. No. It's a real listening skill. It's an affirming thing to people who say, "You know, I'm getting worse, and I can't walk to the bathroom by myself, and I'm not going to make it, then, am I?" And I say, "No, you're not."

Mr. Donahue: And what are you finding now in your communication with people who have come to grips with their impending death?

Ms. Ufema: I find that not many people have come to grips with their impending death and that they—overall, hundreds of people—feel a sense of worthlessness about their lives; they die in a state of depression. I'm finding people who have been yes-men to either their mothers, schools, churches, wives, whomever. They're angry and saying, "Gee, I should have done this or that."

Ms. Albert: I had two children. My son was eight, my daughter was five. And I remember calling a friend of mine who lived at Harrisburg Hospital and I said, "I need to know what to tell my children when I bring my husband home from the hospital because he is already unconscious."

Mr. Donahue: Okay, what is it that Joy did to manifest herself in this terrible dilemma?

Ms. Albert: Well, Joy is a very active, creative listener, and she told me that the children would ask me when they were ready to know, and that I must be honest. And at that time, everything instinctive within me said I wanted to protect these children, and I didn't want to be honest. But I thought that it probably was a good idea. My son said, "When is Daddy going to get well—in about a year?" And I said, "Sometimes doctors can't make people well." And he said, "Do you think Daddy's going to die?" And I said, "I think he is." Then my son said, "Are you going to marry again? And are we going to move?" That told me he already knew, and he had already thought it through so carefully he even knew the consequences. If I had been dishonest, he would have paid. As it was, I was able to say, "We can talk about this." I learned from reading Victor Frankl that if you are going to ask, "Why me?" you must also ask, "Why not me?"

Ms. Ufema: A point here that I think is important is that even though I offered this counselling, Toni could have chosen not to do it. She could have said, "Yes I know you are right, but this is scary and I'm not doing it." Instead, she said, "OK. So it's going to be mean and rough, isn't it?" And I said, "Yes it is, Toni, but I'll tell you what. I'm going to hang in there with you." And that's what it's all about. None of us are getting out of here alive. But what it means is that we are in this together. And I believe that nothing can happen to us as human beings that we haven't been programmed to handle on the planet Earth.

Mr. Donahue: We really do protect the dying, in your view, more than they want to be, is that it? We're stronger than we give ourselves credit for?

Ms. Ufema: Certainly. And we protect, I think, in the name of protecting ourselves.

Mr. Donahue: What has this done for you? Are you at peace with your own mortality?

Ms. Ufema: Sometimes, yes. I probably have other fears more than I fear death. Now some days it's that I fear the dying process, and that it might be painful or very undignified if it takes place in a nursing home. But for the most part, I think I have come to grips with the fact that I must die, and that's sort of in the drawer. So then that means I'm going to live until I die, and I'm going to call my own shots so that when I am dying—not if, when—I can still say, "Hey, you know, for the most part, man, I did it my way."

Ms. Staley: My son was eight and a half when he died of leukemia. He had asked me earlier, "Do I have diabetes?" and I said, "No." Then I told him that he had leukemia. And then it started. He would ask me the questions. He was four when he got sick, and when you're four, what can you know or be told about leukemia or dying? One day he asked me, "Can you die from leukemia?" And I said, "Yes." And we cried, both of us cried, because who wants to tell somebody else that they're going to die? We worked from there on, and up until the last, he wanted to come home to die. He knew he was dying, and he wanted to come home from the hospital.

Mr. Donahue: And what's the lesson you got from this, as his mother?

Ms. Staley: Well, I'm not afraid to die. I feel better about death now than I did before. I think you have to go through something like this to understand it—it makes life different than it was before.

Ms. Ufema: But part of it, I think, Phil, is this: this offering to her and her accepting the challenge. You see, it's always everyone's right to say, "No, I'm afraid I don't want to touch that." And you say, "Hey, wait a second. You have that right to say that, but I'm going to hang in there with you. I'm afraid to watch a little boy I love die, too, but let's go home, Nancy, and do this for him." And it meant that we sat up all night, and that we were tired and hungry and scared and hurting and crying, but we were in there together.

One day Nancy called and said, "Danny wants to talk to you." So he said, "Can I come and ride your horse?" I said, "Yes, have your mom bring you down this afternoon." I hadn't seen him for a while, and when he got out of the car I just had to turn my head because he was looking quite bad. And we saddled up this horse, and that little guy held onto the saddle, Phil. And he could hardly do this. But he wanted that. And so at the deathbed I said to him, "You are getting very close." And Nancy said, "I'm holding your left hand, Danny, and Jesus is holding your right. And at no time before you cross over will you be without somebody holding your hand." I said, "Danny, there are magnificent ponies where you're going." And he wanted to hang glide.

Ms. Staley: I think when the end comes, all in all, you know that you really want them to be taken from you because the suffering and the pain is over. It's very hard. I won't sit here and say that it's easy, and there is nothing to it. But you have to make up your mind that you are going to do something that this person wants. If Danny would not have wanted to come home, we would have stayed in the hospital. I didn't drag him home because I thought this is what I should do.

Ms. Albert: Let me say this. When you go through this experience you begin to realize that death is not the end of life. Life is continuous, and that makes all the difference. It's a different perspective.

Ms. Ufema: Or that death is not the worst thing that could happen. That's what we have to look at. What is the worst thing that could happen? That this little boy is in Room 412 on the pediatric floor and he can't get the cats now, and the doctor is there with the tubes and the whole shooting match, and his mother can't stay overnight. That's the worst thing that could happen.

Ms. Staley: The doctor asked my son if he wanted to go home and he said, "Yes, I do." And the doctor said, "Do you know, Danny, you can have a lot of bleeding and so forth." And Danny said, "Yes." And we took him home anyway. The doctor said to me when he was leaving and writing out the prescriptions, "I'll see you whenever you can't take any more of this. I'll see you back here." And I said to him, "I will not come back here because we're not trying to save his life now."

Mr. Donahue: How do you explain the resistance?

Ms. Ufema: This doctor was a genius. He kept the boy alive for four and a half years because he really knew how to use all these drugs. He was a genius, but he lost the ball game in three minutes at the bedside, and it's because he was hurting. He was losing an eight-year-old after all the energy he put into that.

Audience: I think this matter of dying at home is beautiful, and I commend you. I would like to ask about the questions on the hereafter—where am I going, what's going to happen when I close my eyes and I'm not here anymore—how do you answer that? Do you employ or ask the services of local ministers for that?

Ms. Ufema: It's usually relying on that person's religious concept at that time. Rarely are there deathbed conversions. We die the way we live. The person who dies well is the one who lives congruently. If they have a structure of belief, they live that. If they are atheist and do not believe there is a punitive God later, then they feel all right about dying, and die well.

Audience: How do you help someone who has no specific ideas about what they want or someone who has just given up, knowing that they are going to die?

Ms. Ufema: I support them because that is their right. Few people, however, curl up and die. But for those that do, I support their right to do that. Again, I offer some choices: "Do you want a Polish band and a half a keg of beer? Or do you want to talk to the chaplain—or your sister from Philadelphia?" I give them some specifics to say yes or no to.

Audience: Joy, if a doctor tells you that your loved one is going to die, and the patient does not know it, and the doctor says that he/she feels that the patient should know, do you feel that the family should tell, or do you feel that the doctor should tell them?

Ms. Ufema: It doesn't matter who tells. It matters how.

Mr. Donahue: What do you do if the doctor says, "Don't say anything."

Ms. Ufema: I say, "Listen, I have a responsibility to this individual, and I'm going in there and ask if he wants to talk about how things are going." What to say to people? I simply ask, "Do you feel like sharing with me what it's like being seriously ill?" That gives the patient the control. And then in the development of the relationship you can ask, "What do you want now, and how can I help you help yourself?" And they say, "I'd like my doctor to be more straight with me about this. I don't know if I'm coming or going here or if the medicine's doing any good." Or, "I'd like to go home but my wife does not want me to go home. Should I go back to work? Do I only have a year to live and is it worth working at the American Can Company—or should I take off for Hawaii?" Sometimes people talk about their funeral. That is taking control again.

Mr. Donahue: Can you say what you have learned from all this these past years?

Ms. Ufema: I've learned not to be afraid, and to live my life and be happy with what I do. And when someone comes to the end there's not much you can do but accept it. Can you change a grump in his/her eleventh hour? I think it depends on the person and the outlook they have. We should all be part of the decisions affecting us in our lives. The dying person is at the peak of his vulnerability and it comes down to "What do you want?" Then I do the best I can in the situation.

Reprinted by permission of Multimedia Program Productions.

CHAPTER TEN

Home Care for the Child with Cancer

This study examines the feasibility and desirability of a home care alternative to hospitalization for children with cancer whose cancer control treatment is no longer effective, i.e., children who are dying. Under this option, the parents are the primary providers of their child's care. They are assisted by nurses who consult via telephone and make home visits as necessary. The child's physician serves as a consultant to the family and nurse and prescribes needed medication, especially analgesics. In the first two years of the study, 37 boys and 21 girls died from cancer while participating in home care. Of those 58 participants, 46 died at home, 11 reentered and died in the hospital, and one died in an ambulance en route to the hospital. For the 46 children who died at home, the mean length of involvement from initial nurse contact to time of death was 38.9 days. The mean number of home visits was 13.4, with a mean of 2.2 hours each in duration.

Since 1972 I have been involved in research to identify and evaluate the nursing care required for the family of a child who is dying from cancer at home. The approach utilized has the parent as the primary caregiver, the nurse as a facilitator, and the physician acting as a consultant. The study is entitled, "Home Care for the Child with Cancer" and has several goals:
1. To provide the option of home care to the family of a child with cancer;
2. To assess the home as an alternative care setting for the child with cancer;
3. To determine the role(s) of the nurse in the home care of the child;
4. To identify the most immediate problems of the family and child during home care;
5. To identify the supportive mechanisms required by

the child, the family, and the nurse during their experience of caring for the dying child at home;
6. To identify the benefits and limitations of home care as perceived by the child, the family, the nurse, and other health professionals;
7. To identify the difference in health care costs between care in the home and care in the hospital;
8. To explore the interface of this project with existing health agencies providing services in the home;
9. To assist health care agencies in implementing home care delivery services for a child with cancer.

From August 1976 through June 1978, 58 children have died from their cancers while participating in our project. A more detailed description of the methodology is available elsewhere. The following is an updating of this data:

All of the children with cancer who were referred to the project were accepted. Criteria for referral by the child's physician were: 1) the child is dying, and 2) hospitalization requiring cancer treatment is not planned. A few children in the study received experimental cancer protocols as outpatients but were still expected to die shortly. Most had ceased cancer treatment. Additional criteria identified by the project were: 1) the child's desire to be at home, 2) the parents' desire to care for their child at home, and 3) the parents' recognition of their own ability to care for the child.

During two years of investigation, 46 children (79%) died from their cancers at home; 11 (19%) were readmitted to the hospital and died there, and 1 (2%) died in an ambulance en route to the hospital. For those who did not die at home, the reasons for readmission were for further cancer treatment in one case; pain in two cases; respiratory distress in two cases; hemorrhage, seizures, and an abscess in three separate cases; and in four cases (including the child who died in the ambulance) there was no specific reason. Excluding the child readmitted for cancer treatment, who therefore did not meet the criterion for inclusion in the project, 46 (81%) died at home and 11 (19%) died in the hospital or ambulance.

Approximately half of the children in the project lived in the Minneapolis-St. Paul area, while the other half lived in cities and rural areas throughout Minnesota and neighboring states. The 58 referrals included 31 (53%) from the University of Minnesota Hospitals and 27 (49% from nine other hospitals. A total of 24 different physicians made referrals. 15 (63%) affiliated with the University Hospitals and nine (38%) from other hospitals.

Ages of the children who died at home showed a mean of 9.2 years, and a median of 8.5 years, and ranged from one month to 17 years. The children who died in the hospital (or ambulance) had a mean age of 9.8 years, and a median of 10.5 years, and ranged from three to 17 years of age.

Cancers of 58 children included leukemias, lymphomas, and solid tumors. No single form of cancer has been found to be inappropriate for home care.

Social levels of the household were measured by Hollingshead's index of social position. Occupation and education of the head of household here are combined into a single index. All classes in our study were represented, with about one-third in classes I, II, or III and two-thirds in the lower classes, IV and V.

In providing home care, the child's parents were the primary caregivers, with a nurse facilitating the care as needed. The nurse was on call to make a home visit or for telephone consultation 24 hours a day, seven days a week. The child's physician remained a consultant to the family and nurse. Pain control was a very important factor in caring for the child. Of the 46 children who died at home, all but eight required prescription pain medications. The two children hospitalized for pain control received morphine (IM) or demerol (IM) in the hospital. However, these analgesics were used with children at home. Drugs such as morphine and methadone are not always readily available, e.g., in rural areas, and therefore anticipation of possible need and securing the drugs prior to need was important to many cases.

Specialized equipment and supplies have not been required extensively. For example, of the 46 children who died at home, six required oxygen, four required suction machines, and four required intravenous equipment. However, 24 required no equipment whatsoever. Hospital furnishings, such as wheelchairs, were used by 14 children, and hospital beds by seven children. Interestingly, some children might have been more easily cared for with a hospital bed, but rejected the bed themselves because of its association with hospitalization.

The actual place of death in the home was in a bedroom in 15 (33%) of the cases. The other locations were in the living room, family room, or similar area in the center of household activity.

Duration in the project from first contact to the child's death was a mean of 38.9 days, with a median of 20.5 days, and ranged from one to 256 days. Fifteen children were involved for less than one week; 1] for one to four weeks, 16 for one to three months; and four for over three months. This wide range of times is accounted for by the difficulty in predicting when a child in the terminal stages of cancer will die and by differences among physicians as to when they refer.

Direct professional nurse involvement with the 46 children who died at home entailed a mean of 13.4 visits, and a median of 8.5 visits, and ranged from one to 104 visits per child. The mean length of home visit was slightly over two hours and varied greatly, including some visits which extended for several hours. Such long visits were often at the time of death. There were also a mean of 22.7, a median of 15.5, and a range of zero to 101 telephone conversations between the nurse and family members.

Nurses assigned to each child typically included one nurse who had primary responsibility and one back-up nurse who could take over if the primary was unavailable. In a few cases the role of primary nurse was shared by two, three or even four nurses.

A total of 58 different nurses served as primary or co-primary nurses to the 58 children. For most of the nurses, the home care of a critically ill child was a new experience. All but four of the nurses were R.N.'s. Half of the nurses had baccalaureate degrees. Experience in nursing varied widely; time since receiving the R.N. degree for the 54 registered nurses ranged from one to 44 years.

Looking at the cost of delivery of home care, it should be kept in mind that in this project it was primarily an alternative to hospitalization. At the same time, it would not be valid to assume that each child would have spent an equal amount of time in the hospital had the home care option not been available. A comparison with a similar group of 22 children who died of cancer in the hospital reveal a mean of 29.4 days of final hospitalization compared with a mean of 38.9 days in the home care project. The medians of the home care and the control group are more similar—20.5 and 21.5 days, respectively.

Some of the long-duration home care children would not have been hospitalized for the entire time, especially the 256 days of the longest case. On the other hand, even more of the short-duration children (e.g., one or two days) could probably have left the hospital sooner but were not referred immediately for various reasons.

In comparing costs between hospital and home care, the

basic costs for comparable services were examined. The basic hospital charge for room, board, and nursing services is $200 per day at local hospitals. When the child is at home, the basic cost is for home nursing services. No cost figure is included for the children's room and board in their own home or for care provided the children by their parents. In arriving at an estimate of cost for home nursing services the following schedule was used. Based on local charges for nurse visits of $35 per visit of slightly over an hour in duration, we estimate cost at the rate of $45 per visit for our typically longer visits. That figure includes all nurse salary, mileage, overhead, administration, and minor consumable supplies. Occasionally the home care nurse visited the family during a regularly scheduled clinic visit. Such visits are estimated to be $10 per visit, since they may be of briefer duration and greater convenience to the nurse. Finally, a flat rate of $10 per day for the entire duration in the project was added to the estimate to compensate for being on call 24 hours a day and for telephone consultation. For the 46 children who died at home, the estimated cost using the above rates was a mean of $1,213, a median of $705, and a range of $55 to $7,280. The cost of basic hospitalization at $200 per day for the 22 hospital children would have been a mean of $5,880, a median of $4,300, and a range of $200 to $17,800.

Moreover, the actual cost for the hospitalized children was two to three times as great when the full hospital bill including other charges such as laboratory tests was examined. Complete figures for other costs in home care are not yet finalized, but equipment rental has been modest and laboratory tests have been drastically reduced.

The feasibility of home care for children dying of cancer is clear. Some families may not choose the option, but for those who do, home care has been remarkably effective. Our a priori estimate was that about half of the children would probably die at home when in fact four-fifths of them did so. Caring for a dying child is not easy. It can be physically demanding on the parents, an inconvenience for the nurses, and emotionally draining for all. However, with parents who perceive their own abilities, a professional nurse interested in this form of care, and a physician willing to be flexible in working with the nurse and family, the delivery of home care for dying children was effective in the wide variety of cases studied to date. Fears of inadequacy on the part of parents, failure of the nurse to respond quickly, or lack of understanding of the home care project by the physician may make home care more demanding and increase the probability that the child will be rehospitalized.

The home care option is also desirable. From the standpoint of the most important participants, the dying children, being at home has been universally preferred to hospitalization. The degree of preference for the home was great. In a few cases an almost phobic aversion had developed to the hospital. On the other hand, in one case a child very much liked the hospital, especially several of the staff members, and only slightly preferred being at home. The children must realize that they are receiving good care and would not be better off in the hospital. From the parents' standpoint, home care was viewed as very desirable. The parents could fulfill the child's wish to be at home and could also exercise active control over the situation. The parents were active participants in their child's care and could control the physical environment.

Finally, home care is desirable from an economic standpoint. When the wide range of services available in the hospital is no longer needed and when the parents themselves are the primary caregivers, the cost savings with home care become obvious.

Ida M. Martinson, R.N., Ph.D.

CHAPTER ELEVEN

Suggested Readings

About Dying: An Open Family Book For Parents and Children Together by Sara Bonnett Stein. New York: Walker and Company, 1974.

Why Am I Going To The Hospital? by Carole Livingston and Claire Ciliotta. Secaucus, N.J.: Lyle Straight, 1981.

Explaining Death To Children by Earl Grollman. Boston: Beacon Press, 1967.

Talking About Death: A Dialogue Between Parent and Child by Earl Grollman. Boston: Beacon Press, 1970.

The Bereaved Parent by Harriet Sarnoff-Schiff. New York: Crown Publishers, 1977.

Hope for the Flowers by Trina Paulus. New York: Newman Press, 1972.

Home Care For The Dying Child by Ida Martinson. New York: Appleton-Century-Crofts, 1978.

For Primary-Grade Children: The Tenth Good Thing About Barney by Judith Viorst, and Growing Time by Sandol Warburg.

For Intermediate Grades: Bridge to Terabithia by Katherine Paterson, and Home From Far by Jean Little.

For Upper Grades: Tuck Everlasting by Nancy Babbitt and The Mulberry Music by Doris Orgel.

PART V
A Vision of Hospice

The written word can capture many of the moods and feelings that accompany the death of a family member. But photographs convey something more, the meaning behind the look, the question inherent in the simplest of gestures or actions.

Don Doll, SJ is a professional photographer. During the final months of his mother's life she allowed him to take a few pictures of her and other family members who helped care for her. They are portrayed here along with the text that he wrote to explain the sequence the pictures were taken in.

CHAPTER TWELVE

A Photo Essay by Don Doll, SJ

"Mother, Go in Peace!"

Every day countless families discover that someone close to them has contracted a serious or terminal illness. This is a story of a woman whose family stood by her and cared for her as she made a very difficult decision not to have the brain surgery doctors strongly recommended, whose family stayed at her bedside during her final days in a hospice. It is a beautiful story of how a family who had never experienced any serious illness or death was brought to the point of accepting the death of their wife and mother, and in her final days of commissioning her to go in peace and leave them. It is the story of my mother and my family.

Mother in a spunky mood a Christmas before we knew of her brain cancer; it was a rare occasion when she allowed me to photograph her. She never cared for the way she looked.

A few days before Christmas we learned that she had brain cancer. After some difficult decision making — she declined brain surgery — and during a lull in our conversation I made this photograph.

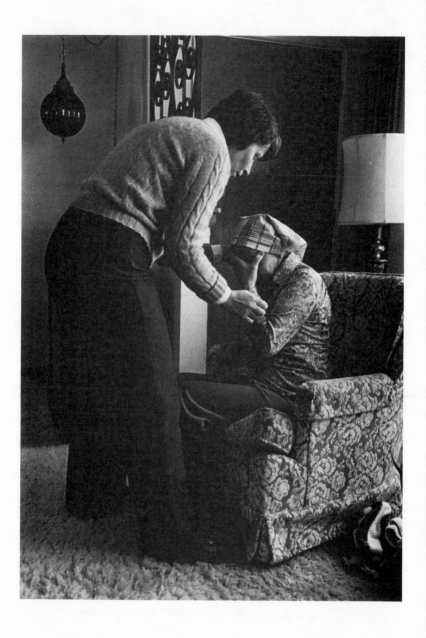

For over three months mother had to be helped every time she had to go to the bathroom. It was extremely painful when she moved her head too quickly.

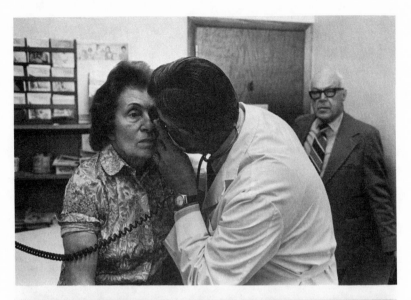

Upper. The brain tumor was gradually pushing those parts of the brain that affect vision and speech. She gradually lost her vision until she was declared legally blind and had great difficulty in carrying on a conversation.

Lower. My sisters Susie and Judy sharing a quiet moment with mother. The doctors had told us it would be a final Christmas we would spend with her so we determined to make it as good as possible.

Upper. After the cobalt therapy, she lost all of her hair. She knew I wanted a photograph of her without her kerchief..

Lower. She experienced moments of intense pain as the brain cancer grew with no place to go.

When I was home, dad could go into the office for a couple of hours. His checking in with her before he left was a scene that I had witnessed many times before. I like the way she is looking at him — with a knowledge and a look that transcends the issue at hand.

This is one of my favorite pictures: to me it represents the domestication of my father at the age of seventy-three when he became the homemaker. Now he had to cook, pay the bills, and clean—all things which he had not done before. It was a rude shock to him especially since he had been preparing for over two decades to die before mother. And now he had to care for her getting up two, three or four times a night.

These two portraits taken three weeks before mother died represent to me the look of a woman who is looking across that chasm which separates those of us who are living from those who have died.

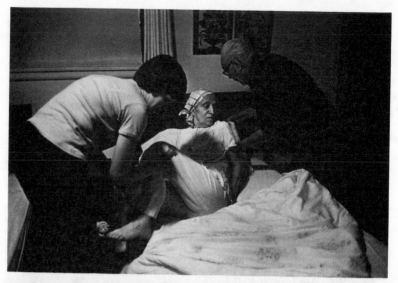

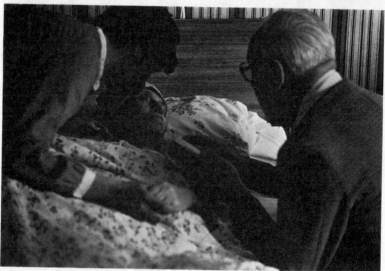

Upper. My father and my sister Sue put mother to bed while she was still at home.

Lower. When my father could no longer care for my mother at home, she agreed to go to a hospice. She didn't want to go. When my father said she could come home when she got better, she replied, "I'm not going to get better." She cried all day long the first day in the hospice — which is not unusual the hospice personnel told us. The next day she stopped eating.

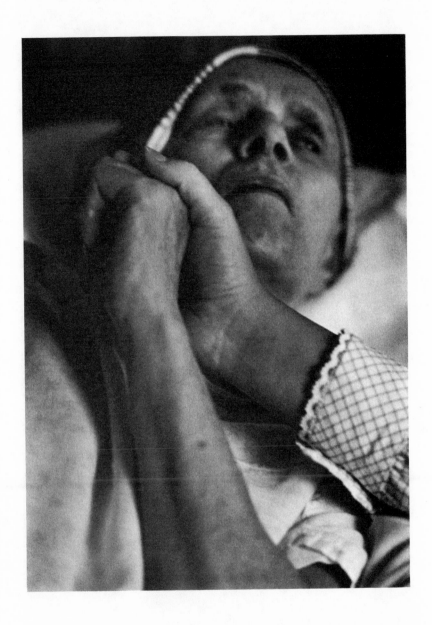

I was called home immediately. When I arrived, they were not expecting her to
live through the evening. She seemed to respond to my voice more than to my
sisters and my father's. At one point my sister Judy whispered into her ear that
"Don's here." She perked up and said, "Oh, for heaven's sake."

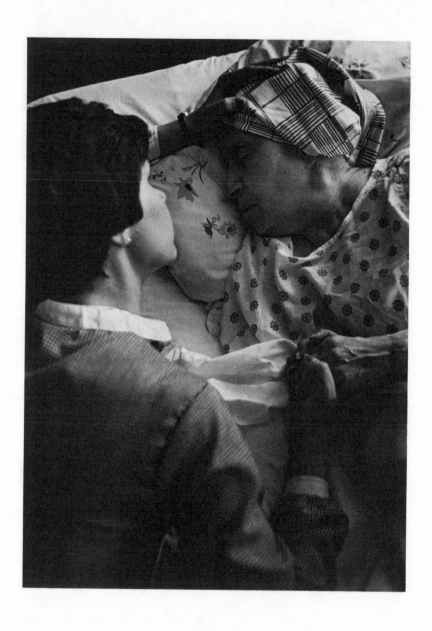

It was a precious time to be with her. We spent long hours sitting by her side. When she awakened we would give her water with a straw. And when we asked her if she would like to pray, we would receive a hoarse "yes."

The turning point for our family at the hospice came after a prayer service. My little sister Susie leaned over and gave mother a big hug and said, "Mother, go in peace." That seemed so right to me; I did the same, and invited my father and sister to do likewise. After that moment, for me there was a sense of resolution. It was like we commissioned her to leave us.

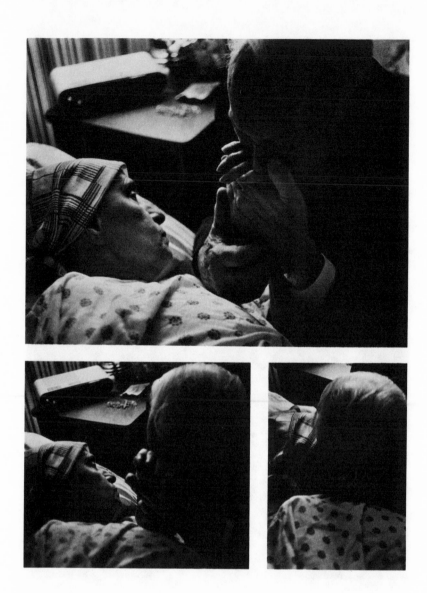

My father saying goodbye to my mother for what he thinks is the last time. Due to her irregular breathing the hospice staff told us that they thought she was going to die that night. As he was extremely tired and exhausted, I insisted that he go home and get a night's rest because I would be maintaining the vigil beside her bedside.

Even though it was very hard on him, dad insisted that I come out and see the marker. I frankly didn't expect him to live after mother died. Though it has been very difficult he is just beginning to adjust after two years.

A few days before this last Christmas, I learned that my mother had brain cancer. After some difficult decision-making—she declined brain surgery—and during a lull in our conversation, I made this photograph.

To explain what it has come to mean to me, I might share a letter I wrote to her.

Dear Mother,

I know that you don't like pictures of yourself, so I better explain why I am sending this one which I did during my visit home.

For me it has all the qualities of a great photograph. One of those qualities is that I can look at it for a long time and always see something new.

I love the way you are looking at me. It is the look of a woman who is deeply at peace with herself and God. It is a look of love at me one of your children. It is both gentle and innocent even though I can see the suffering in your eyes and hands.

I am glad you didn't object this time when I raised my camera. I hope you realize how beautiful you look to me. I shall never forget your loving look. It reminds me of the love you gave to Dad, me, Judy and Sue.

So I hope you can look at this photograph of yourself and see the beauty we see. If this sounds like a love letter, it is.

With very much love,

Don

If I could write a PS to this letter now, I would say:

Mother, through your sickness and death you not only brought us closer together as a family, but you showed us how to face that greatest of unknowns—death. Sue said it best: "After your example, I'm no longer afraid to die." Your role as mother is complete. No mother could hope to give her children more than the example of courage and faith that you gave us.

PART VI
The Law

When a family member is facing the final months of life there is little time to consider legal matters such as will, bank accounts, insurance policies. And yet, the sooner these matters are dealt with, the greater the benefits that result for families. The following pages were not meant to supplant the need to consult with an attorney and complete a will. In most cases that would be the most helpful route to take. What these pages will do is alert the reader to the variety of legal tasks that bear consideration prior to the death of a family member.

CHAPTER THIRTEEN

Legal Considerations

The following matters should be of concern to the patient/client and his/her family during the time of final illness:

I. Whom to Notify:

A. Priest, Minister, or Rabbi.

B. Members of Family.

C. Attorney.

1. If the person has no attorney, the Lawyers Referral Service of the nearest Bar Association will refer you to a panel from whom to choose for this specialty.

Do not hesitate to first inquire as to her/his fees.

2. At the first conference, consider having the members of the family present so all have an understanding as to legal matters.

3. Subsequent conferences may be held between client and attorney alone.

II. Client and Family

A. Client—Is she/he mentally competent?
Does she/he have a guardian?
Limited or General Guardian?

B. Children—If minors, incompetents, or physically or mentally handicapped, consider the person or persons

who will have custody and provide care and maintenance.
Who will act as guardian of such person and/or the
estate?

C. Spouse—Is spouse physically and mentally competent?
Does spouse have a guardian?

III. Assets

Determine location of following documents:

A. Will.

B. Deed to homestead.

C. Deeds to any other real estate in which client has an
interest.
1. Is there property located outside of state?

D. All accounts or credits in his name in banks and/or
lending institutions.

E. Securities.

F. Life insurance policies.

G. Deed to burial plot.

H. Safe deposit box or boxes.

1. Consider obtaining access and removing certain
assets. To protect from later suspicions of relatives or
tax authorities, be careful to determine who goes to the
bank. Best to make complete inventory of box in the
presence of a neutral party (trust or bank officer) and a
family member or members.

2. Consider removing: will and codicils, deed to burial
plot, deeds to real estate, savings passbooks,

securities, and life insurance policies.

3. There might be items in box belonging to others.
a. Consider their removal or at least clearly labelling the ownership. Such items may otherwise be taxable to estate.

I. Savings and Checking Accounts.
1. Checking accounts—consider opening account or accounts in name of spouse to provide ready cash after death to avoid delay in getting accounts released.
2. Consider withdrawing funds from or termination of joint accounts.

J. Automobiles: Titles.
1. Consider avoiding ownership in joint names.
2. Consider having one auto titled in spouse's name alone so it is not part of estate.

K. Recreational motor vehicles (motorcycles, mopeds, boats, snowmobiles, and equipment.)
1. Titles to same.

L. Business interests:

1. Partnership Agreements:
Location of partnership books and records.

2. Sole Proprietorship:
Location of books and records.

3. Close Corporation:
Location of books and records. Any buy and sell agreements.

M. Profit-sharing Plans.

N. Pension Plans.

1. Any benefits payable after death.

2. To whom—Maybe provision for beneficiary needs

updating.

O. Trusts created by client.

P. Trusts in which client is beneficiary.

Q. Interest in any unsettled estate.

R. Any assets held by third person for safekeeping or for any other reason.

S. Copies of income tax returns.

T. Any power of attorney.

U. Any ante-nuptial or post-nuptial agreement.
1. Should be reviewed.

V. Individual Retirement Account—IRA.

W. Keogh Plan for self-employed or for client himself as partner.

IV. Liabilities

A. Mortgage on home and/or other real estate.

B. Mortgage on automobiles, furniture, recreational vehicles, boats, etc.

C. Charge accounts, outstanding bills for repairs or improvements to real estate, etc.

D. Is there mortgage insurance covering balance due upon death?

E. Is client divorced or legally separated? Consider obligation for payment of alimony and support and property settlement.

V. Power of Attorney

A. Is there a power of attorney in existence?
1. Is it valid?

B. Consider granting power of attorney to an individual. Take care in selection of the person to act. Such person is known as attorney-in-fact for the grantor of this power.

1. Grantor must be competent.

2. Grantor may still act on his behalf without consulting attorney-in-fact even though there is power of attorney in existence.

3. Power of attorney ceases upon death or incompetency of grantor.

4. Don't use printed forms. This is an important document. Consult the attorney.

5. Can be for general or for limited purposes.

6. Can provide for:

a) transactions of all banking business, endorsing and depositing checks, and cash and withdrawing funds by check or otherwise;

b) transfer or disposition of assets;

c) access to safe deposit box or boxes;

d) amending insurance policies;

e) dealing with securities and leases;

f) dealing with nursing or retirement homes and others. Consenting to medical and/or surgical techniques or procedures.

7. Grantor and attorney-in-fact must complete and sign forms of all bank and savings and loan accounts and safe deposit boxes.

8. May be revoked by grantor at any time.

9. May have alternate attorney-in-fact.

VI. Guardianship

A. If there is a question as to competency, consider petition to the local probate court under procedure outlined in state law.

VII. Conservatorship

A. This may be preferable over guardianship if person is competent.

B. The person himself petitions the court requesting court to appoint person to act as his conservator.

C. Used where person wants someone to handle his financial and business affairs.

D. Conservator does not have control or custody of the person.

VIII. Review Will and Codicils

A. There may be change in family or financial situations since client signed will or codicil and testator may want to make changes.

1. Possibly personal representative is deceased or no longer available.

2. Death of a beneficiary.

3. Are witnesses to existing will available to testify?

4. May be other reasons to update will.

IX. If No Will

A. Serious consideration should be given to executing a will.

B. <u>Caveat</u>: Don't use printed forms. This can prove dangerous in many ways.

C. Have attorney draft the will and be present at its execution.

D. The drafting of a will involves the making of decisions and taking steps requiring professional judgment which can be obtained only by years of training, experience, and study. Only the practicing lawyer can avoid the innumerable pitfalls and advise the course best suited for individual situation.

E. Before conference on will with attorney, prepare a list of names, addresses of next of kin (if minor—date of birth), and list of assets.

F. Determine state of residency of proposed testator. The following criteria apply: Residency shown on tax return; car licenses, and hunting licenses, and where registered to vote.

X. Life Insurance Policies

A. Should review.

B. Is it still in force?

C. What is face value? Are there any loans outstanding?

D. What are premiums? Who will now pay them?

E. Who are primary and secondary beneficiaries?

1. To change beneficiary, you must obtain the correct forms from each insurance company.

2. In emergency, you can send certified letter changing beneficiary signed by client and addressed to insurance company's general counsel.

F. Who owns the policy?

G. Some lapsed policies can be reinstated without evidence of insurability.

H. If any questions, consult with insurance agent or insurance company representative.

I. Dividends on permanent policies may be used to purchase additional insurance. Either pay the gross premiums or elect automatic premium loan.

J. Possibly purchase paid-up additions to policy with accumulated dividends.

K. Maybe convert to permanent coverage a non-renewable policy which may soon lapse.

L. Consider converting decreasing term to permanent coverage provided there is no loss of protection in so doing.

XI. Income Tax

A. If over 55 years of age, may wish to take advantage of exclusion of up to $100,000.00 of gain on sale of principal residence from gross income.

B. This can provide liquidity for paying bills now or at death.

XII. Other Matters

A. Hospital and medical policies.

B. Directions pertaining to body and organs. Should complete proper forms obtained from recipient school or organizations.

C. Does person desire autopsy? If autopsy performed, usually medical schools will refuse to take body. However, the same may not apply to organs.

D. If under Title XIX, consider $1,500.00 irrevocable burial trust.

E. If client is trustee of a trust, consider providing for successor if none already provided for.

F. If client is co-fiduciary, consider his resignation.

G. If client is guardian for anyone, or acting in any fiduciary capacity, determine whether he should render accountings in fiduciary capacities in which he is acting.

H. Jointly owned real and personal property—Where held in the names of one or more persons in joint tenancy with right of survivorship, it is advisable that the person prepares and executes a sworn statement in the form of an affidavit setting forth the amount of contributions by himself and other joint tenants toward the acquisition of such jointly owned real and personal property. This should be accomplished prior to death in order to satisfy the taxing authorities after death.

I. There are ethical considerations involved with two extremes: Preserve life at all costs and with all means at our disposal versus terminate life when it becomes dysfunctional and burdensome in a serious way.

Nicholas G. Ewens

CHAPTER FOURTEEN

How to Run Your Life When You're Left Alone

In reading the April-May issue of <u>Modern Maturity</u>, I was struck with the advice that "widows must take time over decisions." If my years as a widow can help even one other person retain sanity, solvency, and good spirits, I'd like to help.

I was saved from making major errors by a good friend who worked for a lawyer. She advised me when I was widowed that I should postpone any major changes in my lifestyle for at least a year. And I owe her much for this advice.

My children were super—none more honest and none more caring. But I shudder to think where (or what) I would be now had I taken their advice.

"Sell your house and rent an apartment." "Sell your house and move in with me." I was so bewildered (my husband's death was sudden) that I didn't know which way to go. Thanks to my friend's advice, I did nothing.

If I had sold my house the money would have gone toward apartment rent that—with inflation—would have far exceeded the mortgage payments I make now. If I had moved in with my son, who had three darling children at the time, either I'd have gone berserk or we might have established lasting enmity. The kids are in their teens now and the house is full.

Dad can yell, "Turn off that noise!" but Grandma can't (or shouldn't). Mother can say, "You shouldn't wear so much makeup!" but if Grandma does, she's called an old fogy—and perhaps she is.

I repeat. Don't make decisions for at least a year.

Your husband probably had "his" chair in the living room or den. It's hard to look at now.

Rearrange the furniture, then you sit in the chair. It's probably the most comfortable one in the house anyway, and you won't envision him in it every time you look up.

If sitting at the dining table alone brings on a crying spell, find a small table, put it in a pleasant spot, and serve your meals there.

Prepare real meals. No snacks, no "just a bite of toast and tea"—or your children will have to take over. If you're used to making meat and potatoes or the "same old thing," try some gourmet recipes. They're surprisingly cheap if you use the right ones, and their preparation will take up a lot of your empty time.

If you have too much after you've cut down the recipe, eat what you can and freeze the rest; better yet, call a friend in for lunch.

Of course, everyone by now has told you to find an outside interest. The one in which I found my greatest rewards, most freedom, and reasonable wage (since I'm not inclined to working for charity) is babysitting. Try it, if you like children at all. I, personally, have sat through a family of four boys—the oldest now 24—and feel like one of the family.

Don't limit yourself to just one thing. Working a little has given me enough extra income so that I can now do a bit of travelling. I trade cars every three years and have time to spend with my own family. But not so much that they get bored with me, or I with them.

All in all, I now have a very full and rewarding life.

If I had turned my finances over to my son—as many suggested at my husband's death—I would have to ask him every time I wanted to take a trip, go to a play, or buy a car. He wouldn't necessarily have said no. But to have my son say, "At your age?" if my whim was to buy a sports car would have taken a lot of joy out of a life I've handled well since the initial shock of my husband's death.

I'm my own woman now, and hope the day never comes when I have to lose my independence.

Again, I say thanks for my friend's advice, which helped me keep that independence.

Myrtle Krueger

CHAPTER FIFTEEN

Coping: Insurance Need Not Lapse

Pete was laid off in September. He wrote to the state insurance commissioner's office when he learned his wife was pregnant with twins. Was there any way he could get health insurance? He would have had insurance if he hadn't been laid off.

Dave, 64, wrote to the commissioner saying he had cancer and needed to retire from his job. Was there any way he could continue his group health insurance?

Janet, who was insured under her husband's group health insurance, worried that she would have to go without health insurance after their divorce until she found a job.

There is a happy ending for each of these stories, however.

Pete, Dave, and Janet are able to maintain their health coverage simply by picking up the insurance premiums themselves. The chance to do so should have been offered to Pete when he was laid off. His employer needed to be reminded of a change in state law. And so, Dave and Janet will get their opportunities to continue coverage as well.

In a little-noticed move, a Wisconsin state law was changed last year to require that continued group coverage be offered to Pete, Dave, and Janet and people like them. While this change pleases some employers who can offer sound health insurance coverage, other employers object to the extra book work the change requires.

Look for a move in the Legislature this year to try to change the law before it becomes widely understood and accepted.

Group hospital and medical policies now must allow continued coverage for 12 months to many people if they pay the appropriate premiums to the employer.

Any policy issued or renewed after May 13, 1980, in Wisconsin must contain the change. The change actually allows the person involved to choose continued coverage or the more expensive move of converting the policy to an individual policy approved by the state insurance commissioner. In most instances, the better choice would be to continue the group insurance. The person who does choose continuation keeps the right to convert the policy at the end of a year. People included are:
A former spouse of an employee whose coverage would otherwise be ended because of divorce or annulment; an employee whose coverage would otherwise end because he or she is retiring or being laid off or taking sick leave or a leave of absence. (The change specifically does not include those discharged from employment for misconduct in connection with employment); the spouse or dependent of an employee whose coverage would otherwise be terminated because of the employee's death. The employer has an obligation to notify the individual of his continuation and conversion rights. Until this notification is given, the individual has the right to continue under the group policy by paying the regular premium otherwise paid by the employer. That obviously does mean extra work for the employer who in previous times probably would have crossed the names off the books immediately.

Nationally, one out of eight persons does not have health insurance for one reason or another. The National Center for Health Services Research estimated in 1977 that 26.6 million people—or 12.6% of the non-institutionalized population—did not have health insurance.

There are no such figures available for Wisconsin, but the national figures have been used in other states that have passed similar legislation. Insurance policies are regulated by individual states, not by the federal government.

Another change is taking effect this year. Health insurance companies must offer high-risk health insurance plans. The concept is similar to high-risk auto insurance, and it is for a person who has been turned down for health coverage by two companies. While the cost will not be low, the premium may not exceed 130% of the premium for standard coverage during the first three years.

Just to give you some more perspective about the cost of health care and the importance of insurance, Wisconsin hospitals charge roughly $1,800 for an average stay. Add to that the charges by the doctors who handle the case.

Mildred Freese

Reprinted with permission from The Milwaukee Journal, January 12, 1981

CHAPTER SIXTEEN

Suggested Readings

Wisconsin Probate Manual: A Manual for Assisting in The Informal Probating of an Estate. Wisconsin Citizens for Legal Reform. Inc., 7230 W. Capitol Drive. Milwaukee, Wisconsin 53216, 1975. $2.25.

PART VII
Funerals, Wills, and the Living

No one likes to plan a funeral, or even to think about attending one. This chapter presents the options that families can consider, from a traditional funeral service to handling the majority of arrangements themselves. Funeral directors are able to assist them, as are clergy men and women and hospice staff members. Many families hesitate to do anything about funeral plans until the last possible moment. These pages are meant to facilitate advance thinking and planning about details that are otherwise left to the decisions of people not connected with them on a regular basis.

CHAPTER SEVENTEEN

Making Funeral Arrangements

It is difficult to think about one's own funeral or that
of someone else dear to us. Most people put it off until
they are at the worst possible time for decision-making,
namely within a few hours or days after the death of a
loved one. This is understandable, and will likely
continue to be the case for the foreseeable future.
However, sooner or later, a person reaches the day
when the settling of these difficult, delicate arrangements must be faced. This article, and the one
immediately following, are offered as guides for
families who need background information on the types
of decisions to be made and the range of options that
are available to them.

I. Assistance from Friends

At a time of loss we need others near who can assist us
in thinking clearly amid great emotion. Various people
can serve in this capacity—a spouse, a brother or sister,
parents, a pastor, neighbors, friends, adult children. But
it is important to choose at least one person who is
objective to the situation, so that their suggestions can
offer the balance and clarity that is not easily achieved
by grieving family members. This is particularly true
when it comes to visiting the funeral parlor and making
the central decisions about a casket, the type of
service, the other details that will honor the body and
the spirit of the deceased person.

It is essential that family members discuss major
decisions at home, before they send one or two
representatives off to the funeral parlor. This can be a
means of avoiding family disputes later on and also
ensure participation by family members for each aspect
of the arrangements. This is time-consuming, and it is

difficult to bring together everyone on short notice. Perhaps a list can be made of the items that are most significant, and then discussion can occur on each of them: will there be traditional services or something tailored to the uniqueness of this person; what type of casket is desired; is cremation a possibility or will there be burial beneath the ground; where will the wake occur, and what visiting hours will be established; will friends be invited to a meal or other type of gathering after the funeral? As families discuss these questions they will come to understand the extent of the items to be settled and the general style of service that seems most appropriate to commemorate this person's life. In cases where the person left behind, either orally or in writing, prior instructions about the funeral arrangements, families will be wise to give these considerations the utmost attention and respect. Again, a person outside of the family structure can provide much assistance in both the discussion of these issues and the decisions that are made about them.

II. What Comes First

When a person who has been sick over many months does die, families have advance time for planning particular details. When a death is sudden and unexpected, it is much more difficult to gather the necessary people together to settle central issues. In both cases these things will have to be considered:

A. Who needs to be notified about the death: relatives, those living out of town, business and social friends. A list should be made and the calls divided up among those who are most able to relate this sad news in a sensitive way.

B. In some circumstances, particularly if the person died in a hospital, permission may be requested to perform an autopsy. Families are usually very free to say yes or no to this request, but it should be discussed by them—and can sometimes be settled prior to the actual death.

C. If a church or synagogue will be used, someone must find out when the building will be available; this also applies to the minister, priest, or rabbi who may conduct the service.

D. A notice in the newspaper—this gives public notice of the death and the date and time of the wake and funeral. Families are able to include any facts that they wish, but they should realize that there is a charge of approximately $100 for the typical size death notice. Evening newspapers often have 9:00 a.m. limits for their notices, while morning papers set a 5:00 p.m. limit.

E. Place and time of burial—many cemeteries are closed by noon on Saturday and on holidays. There is an obligatory 48-hour waiting period before a cremation can be completed.

F. The question of whether there will be an open or closed casket should be freely discussed by families. A decision about pallbearers will also need to be made—men and women are now able to be used for this role. Memorial gifts in lieu of flowers may be the wish of either the deceased or some members of the family.

G. The choice of a funeral home—many families are accustomed to relying on the help of one in their neighborhood. Time, geography, and financial issues should be kept in mind when making this decision.

The article by Thomas Reese in Chapter Twenty provides detailed information about each of these areas. Families are encouraged to discuss them together, and then to consult with a funeral director for additional help. They are trained to obtain necessary information for an obituary notice, the facts required on a death certificate, and the regulations of local cemeteries and crematoria. Families who wish to handle some or all of these details by themselves can benefit by reading the article that describes what the Phillips family did for the funeral of their father.

III. Matters of Preference

Funerals can be held in churches, cemeteries, funeral homes, and private homes. They can be traditional, personal, religious, or non-sectarian. They can occur within a few hours or days of the person's death, or they can be held a week or two later (when cremation has been chosen or the body has been donated to science). The purpose of this chapter is to alert people to the choices and options that they are able to set up on their own, no matter what type of funeral service is decided upon.

A. <u>Wakes</u> can be held over several days' time, in one evening or morning, with set prayers and rituals followed, or with variations planned by the family. Some families designate one member to give a brief summary of the person's life and accomplishments. Others encourage visitors to sit down and share in the memories and experiences they had with the person during his/her life. Music, either taped or live, by a soloist, choir, or all who come, can be a benefit during the wake. In past decades most wakes occurred in the home. Some churches today encourage their members to use the church and the church basement for this gathering. Funeral homes and cemeteries also provide ample space, depending on the number of friends expected to come.

B. The <u>Funeral</u> <u>Service</u>—Most families prefer to have the religious professionals plan the ceremony, but even in these cases there is ample room for family participation. The choice of songs (and the organ, guitar, flute, or other instruments to be used) can be planned by one or more family members. The choice of readers and the primary celebrant can also be made by the family, as can the person chosen to give the main talk or sermon. Particular tasks such as bringing up candles or flowers, placing items of remembrance on the altar or entrance table, handing out song sheets can frequently be done by relatives or children not immediately involved in the family's loss. Those family members who are asked to read at a funeral or to deliver an address should be cautioned that their emotions may well be stronger than they expect, and that they should not accept the task unless they are prepared to deal with the outbreak of tears that may occur. Also, people not trained to use microphones will need to practice speaking into them before the service is held.

C. A Time To Share—What people say after the loss of a friend is much less important than their presence and support. This can be expressed through cards, the bringing of food to a family, babysitting help, picking up out-of-town guests, handling incoming telephone calls. Some churches and synagogues have regular com- mittees set up to prepare a meal for those attending the funeral. This can be a good opportunity for all concerned to relax and share their grief together. A meal at a restaurant after the burial can also provide this type of outlet, as can a family inviting people back to a central home for this purpose.

D. Donation of Organs—The use of organs and bodies for transplants, education, and research is a way that some people choose to assist others through their death. The most comprehensive information on this subject and others related with funerals can be obtained from the Continental Association of Funeral and Memorial Societies at Suite]]00,]828 L St., N.W., Washington, D.C. 20036. Their booklet entitled A Manual of Death Education and Simple Burial is available for $2.00 from this address, and will also provide other local informa- tion for making arrangements.

The living can be helped through the donation of body parts such as kidneys, skin, corneas, heart, pituitary gland. Reseach can benefit from permission to make use of the heart muscle, ovaries, liver, lungs, ear bone, or the entire cadaver for further study.

Many people carry a uniform donor card in their wallet or on their driver's license. This is legal authorization for all anatomical gifts in the United States, and it may specify donation of any particular organ or one's entire body. Two witnesses need to sign the card to make it legal.

Over 35,000 people a year could be cured of blindness if more corneas were available for transplant. This gift can be given whether the person who died had good or poor eyesight. It can also be arranged after he has died, but the local eye bank must be notified and come to remove the corneas within four to six hours after the death occurs.

Kidney transplants can make a normal life possible for the 40,000 people who have chronic renal disease and must depend on a dialysis machine to stay alive. It is preferable for this surgery to be agreed upon before the death occurs because the operation must be carried out within a short time of death for it to have a high chance of success for the recipient of the kidney.

E. Bequeathal of Bodies—When a body is donated to a medical school there is usually no cost to the family. Staff from the school will come to the hospital or the home to transport the body, and are available 24 hours a day, seven days a week. Most medical schools prefer the completion of their own bequeathal forms before death, but some are willing to have the papers signed after the death occurs. Alternative plans should also be made by the family, even when a body has been donated, because most medical schools will not accept a body if it has been in an accident or a fire, or if an autopsy has been performed. Also, a body will be accepted after a cornea transplant, but not if kidneys or other organs have been donated. Most Protestant,

Catholic, and Jewish groups approve and encourage donations, with the Orthodox Jewish faith the principal exception.

IV. The Overriding Concern

At a time of loss many people feel helpless to make the types of decisions that are required of them. They want to do "the right thing" but they are so overwhelmed by their grief that they have neither the energy nor the time to take the necessary steps. It helps to realize that each funeral, each burial, is special for this person and this family. Rituals and customs established over decades and generations suggest how to approach many of the key issues involved. They should be honored and taken into account, but so, too, should the needs and styles of those who are most affected by the death.

When a person dies, whether at home or in a hospital, there is no immediate need to do anything other than express one's grief and pain. If this takes several hours and if other family members need to be contacted, then let it take several hours. The worst that can happen has happened, so all else can be rearranged to fit into the response that occurs to the death. A pastor or rabbi can lend valuable assistance at this time, as can neighbors and other friends who are willing to help—provided that they are given particular tasks to do.

These pages suggest some of the alternatives to be considered. Families should use them to imagine and plan other approaches that will embody and express their love and remembrance of this particular person. The "rightness and wrongness" of these plans can only be judged and measured by those family members and friends who were closest to the person who died.

CHAPTER EIGHTEEN

A Living Will

In many states the practice of drawing up "a living will" has come to be commonplace. It is meant to provide help to family members, friends, and physicians who may need to make decisions about artificial life support systems in the face of impending death. Some parts of the country have passed "living will legislation," while others have not. However, when disagreement does arise over the type of medical treatment to be utilized when a person is near death and unable to make decisions by him/herself, the evidence of a written document does carry great impact for those left with making the decision. Here is a sample living will:

To My Family, My Physician, My Lawyer, and All Others Whom It May Concern:

Death is as much a reality as birth, growth, maturity, and old age—it is the one certainty of life. If the time comes when I can no longer take part in decisions for my own future, let this statement stand as an expression of my wishes and directions, while I am still of sound mind.

If at such a time the situation should arise in which there is no reasonable expectation of my recovery from extreme physical or mental disability, I direct that I be allowed to die and not be kept alive by medications, artificial means, or "heroic measures." I do, however, ask that medication be mercifully administered to me to alleviate suffering even though this may shorten my remaining life.

This statement is made after careful consideration and is in accordance with my strong convictions and beliefs. I want the wishes and directions here expressed carried out to the extent permitted by law. Insofar as they are not legally enforceable, I hope that those to whom this will is addressed will regard themselves as morally bound by these provisions.

Date _____

Witness_____

Signed_____

Witness_____

Copies of this request have been given to: _____

Declarants may wish to add specific statements to the living will to be inserted in the space provided for that purpose above the signature. Possible additional provisions are suggested below:

1. I appoint_____ to make binding decisions concerning my medical treatment.

or

I have discussed my plans as to life-sustaining measures with the following who understand my wishes:

2. Measures of artificial life support in the face of impending death that are especially abhorrent to me are:

A. Electrical or mechanical resuscitation of my heart when it has stopped beating.

B. Nasogastric tube feedings when I am paralyzed and no longer able to swallow.

C. Mechanical respiration by machine when my brain can no longer sustain my own breathing.

D._____

3. If it does not jeopardize the chance of my recovery to a meaningful or sentient life or impose an undue burden on my family, I would like to live out my last days at home rather than in a hospital.

4. If any of the tissues are sound and would be of value as transplants I freely give my permission for such donation.

Sign and date before two witnesses to ensure that you are not under pressure. Send a copy to several family members and to your physician. Discuss your intentions now with those closest to you. Look over your living will once a year and redate it to make it clear that your wishes are unchanged.

Reprinted with permission from Concern For Dying, An Educational Council,
250 W. 57th St.,
New York, N.Y. 10019.

CHAPTER NINETEEN

He Was Buried As He Wished

Eugene Philipp's funeral this week went the way he planned—at the hands of those who loved him.

His six sons built a plywood casket in his garage and tenderly placed his body in it. They lifted it into the crematory chamber themselves and closed the door. They carried the cremation canister to the cemetery, placed it in the small hole and covered it with dirt themselves.

"He was handled by those he loved, all the way through," said his wife Joan.

And in handling the funeral themselves—much as deaths were handled years ago—the family found strength to help them face the hardest part of all, saying good bye to their 59-year-old father and husband.

"It was a very moving experience, one that was filled with grief," said his son Joseph, 30, of Houston, Texas. "But the experience allowed us to work through that grief. It was a very personal family experience."

Philipp died in his wife's arms September 27 at Columbia Hospital, after suffering from leukemia for more than four years. He had entered the hospital September 5 for treatment and died after his lungs filled with fluid.

While his death came sooner than family members expected, they were not unprepared to carry out Philipp's wishes to have his funeral handled without the help of a funeral director. He had researched the matter carefully last winter and written a page of instructions, including telephone numbers and names of officials to contact to fill out the necessary forms.

Wisconsin law permits family members to handle the funeral of a close relative without going through a funeral director.

"His list was very accurate," said Mrs. Philipp, 51.

Following his instructions, she and another son, John, 22, went to Milwaukee City Hall to obtain a death certificate. After having it signed by Philipp's physician, they took it to the Medical Examiner's Office for cremation authorization.

They then went back to City Hall for a burial permit and burial transit permit. Appointments were made for cremation at Wisconsin Memorial Park and burial of the ashes at the veterans' cemetery here. An autopsy was performed on the body, which was stored at Columbia during the 48 hours required by law before cremation can take place.

"It wasn't as hard to do as I had thought," said Mrs. Philipp. "It was a very positive thing. It was what he wanted."

In addition to legal considerations, Philipp also had included details for building the casket: "Construct wooden box, 6 feet by 2 feet by 1½ feet high...with lid...cheapest lumber possible."

A third son, Timothy, 26, of Milwaukee, masterminded the actual construction. Because he wasn't sure whether the dimensions referred to the inside or outside of the box, he measured one of his brothers to find out how much space was needed to hold a body.

He found some plywood in the garage of the family's Whitefish Bay home, left over from a construction project years ago, and spent $13.99 on other necessary lumber and nails. Handles were made out of clothesline that cost $1.49.

A cedar cross, made by the oldest son, Eugene Jr., 31, was placed on the outside of the casket, which was painted white and lined with a white sheet.

On Monday, after borrowing a station wagon, the family went to the hospital to pick up Philipp's body. The sons lifted it carefully into the casket.

"We looked at him and covered him and prayed over him," said Mrs. Philipp. "Then everybody helped nail the lid on. Everyone helped."

They drove to Wisconsin Memorial Park, where even Philipp's three and a half-year-old grandson, who had asked to participate, helped slide the casket into the crematory.

Then they left, gathering together at the Wauwatosa home of Eugene Jr. They shared a meal and spent the afternoon reminiscing until it was time to return for the box containing Philipp's cremated remains.

"We handled that box as carefully as when he was alive," said Mrs. Philipp. "Because that's what I did when he was alive. He wanted the hands that loved him to hold him."

On Tuesday, they were alone as they buried the ashes. They shared prayers and readings. Then Joseph put the canister in the ground and everyone threw some dirt over it.

"Somehow we had a sense of togetherness, and togetherness with him," said Joseph. "I think we had a sense that he was with us."

The family also helped plan a memorial mass for Philipp, which was held Thursday night at St. Monica's Catholic Church in Whitefish Bay. Four of the sons gave brief recollections of their father, whose closing words in his instructions were aimed at them: "Keep your cool. Don't panic. Pray for YOURSELF!!"

And through all the activities of laying him to rest, it was obvious that his influence still penetrated the family he had led.

"Through all these days, the joys of my father, and the memories, have been able to come through the grief," said Timothy. "And I think it's safe to say that this can be a joyful time."

"I think somehow our personal involvement was a big help," said Mrs. Philipp, "because we didn't stand and watch and wonder what was going on. Somehow we're sure he knows about everything. And yes, (he would be) pleased. Very pleased."

Barbara Koppe

Reprinted with permission from The Milwaukee Journal, October, 1979

CHAPTER TWENTY

Burying A Loved One

While a family is still in the depths of its grief, it must weigh the advice of funeral directors and requirements of church and civil law. Misconceptions and misrepresentations are all too common.

At some point in your life, you will probably have to deal with a funeral parlor to prepare for burial a friend or relative. Someday, someone will have to do the same for you. With the average cost of a funeral over $2,000, for many families this will be the third most costly purchase—after buying a home and a car—you or your loved ones will make. But the arrangements are usually made with much less thoughtful consideration than the costs warrant. The deceased's family are not in a position to make very intelligent decisions because of grief, time pressures for arranging the funeral, and general lack of knowledge about death-related legal and religious requirements.

Most families depend on the funeral director's advice and counsel for the funeral. But the Federal Trade Commission (F.T.C.) has found that many members of this $6.4 billion industry take advantage of the family's grief and ignorance and, like maggots, live off the dead.

Many funeral directors, for example, refuse to give specific price information over the telephone or in the funeral home until after a purchase has been made. Some directors fail to inform families accurately about the legal requirements for funeral merchandise such as coffins or for services such as embalming.

These directors are, of course, a disgrace to the industry and perhaps a small minority, but the industry itself has done little to discourage them. In fact, it has actively opposed attempts by the F.T.C. to stop these abuses through regulations.

The industry argues that the abuses are not widespread and that consumers are in fact well treated by funeral homes. A survey sponsored by the National Funeral Directors' Association found that 88 percent of the respondents were very satisfied with the funeral director's service, and 90 percent thought the funeral director adequately explained the choices the consumer could make. The F.T.C. felt, however, that consumer satisfaction was not a good indicator of abuses because purchasers frequently do not know what is being done to them.

My own experience with the funeral industry when my father died confirms the findings of the F.T.C. Luckily, my father had threatened to come back and haunt us if we dared have anything but the cheapest funeral possible. Such instructions from the deceased—preferably in writing and filed away with his will—are extremely important in alleviating guilt feelings. It is difficult to deal with an irrational relative who wants to give nothing but the best—the most expensive—to the deceased. The only definitive antidote to such nonsense is the expressed wishes of the deceased.

When I saw the funeral director, I explained that my mother wanted my father's body cremated. "Oh, we can have that done, but I won't guarantee that the Catholic cemetery will accept the ashes." Since I was a priest, I told him I would take care of that. Since the body was to be cremated, I saw no reason to have it embalmed or put in a coffin. "No, I'm sorry, but the law requires embalming and a casket." Thus, rather than being cheaper, I found that cremation was going to cost as much as a regular funeral plus $50 for the crematory. Finally we picked out the second cheapest coffin in the showroom. The cheapest was a disgusting pink, and I did not care what my father said, he was not going to be buried in that!

I later found out, while reading the F.T.C. June 1978 study of funeral industry practices, that I had been subjected to a classic case of the way in which many funeral directors treat their customers. While laws governing the care of the dead vary from state to state, in general here are some things you should know about them before you see a funeral director.

Embalming. Prior to the Civil War, embalming was not commonly practiced in this country. Embalming began at that time in order to preserve the bodies of deceased soldiers so that they could be shipped home. In earlier times, it was common for members of the family or friends to wash and prepare the body for burial. Frequently a member of the family or the local carpenter would make the coffin.

Today, according to the F.T.C., "No state has an absolute legal requirement that remains must be embalmed in all circumstances. The special circumstances under which embalming may be required include death by communicable disease, interstate transportation, holding the body beyond a specified length of time and, in Kansas, burial in a mausoleum and intercounty transportation of the remains."

Embalming has been defended by some in the funeral industry as a public health measure. But the F.T.C. reported: "A review of the evidence suggests that the empirical basis for the public health necessity claimed for embalming is at best dubious." Dr. Bruce Dull, assistant director for programs at the Public Health Service's Center for Disease Control, said: "We have yet to see any data indicating that there is a public health problem in the United States today associated with unembalmed or ineffectively embalmed cadavers."

Even the embalming of those who have died of communicable disease has been criticized by public health officials. "In those few cases where a person dies of a highly infectious disease," commented a

British Columbia Department of Health official, "a far better procedure would be to wrap and securely seal the body in heavy plastic sheeting before removing it from the room where death occurred." The City of Vancouver Health Department reached a similar conclusion: "There does not seem to be any indication that embalming is necessary from the public health point of view, except when it is necessary to preserve the body for some time, for example, to permit its shipment abroad for disposal."

There is, of course, no religious requirement for embalming. In fact, it is forbidden by Orthodox Jews, who consider it a desecration of the dead. Thus, the women who came to Jesus' tomb on Easter morning came to anoint his body with spices but not to embalm it.

Some funeral directors have falsely claimed that embalming would protect the deceased from decay forever. But the purpose of embalming is really only to preserve the body for a short period of time. No matter how well-embalmed, the body will eventually decay. At best, it will end up looking like King Tut—not a pretty sight once the gold and jewels are removed.

The F.T.C. is considering requiring funeral directors to provide a written statement explaining that embalming would not prevent the eventual decay of the deceased's body. The funeral industry objects to such a requirement, and the staff of the F.T.C. is having trouble drafting a statement that might not be offensive and distasteful to the deceased's family. The F.T.C. rule does forbid any misrepresentation of or using sealed (supposedly watertight or airtight) caskets, but this rule is more difficult to enforce.

Caskets. The casket is usually the most expensive item purchased for the funeral. Since funeral homes make a commission from the sale of caskets, they give careful consideration to how the caskets are presented to their customers. The F.T.C. found that many funeral homes display their cheapest casket in a soiled condition or in an unattractive color.

Worse yet, many do not even put their cheapest coffin in the showroom. As a Texas state legislator explained: "The family sees that apparently the cheapest priced casket and service is $600. How is the family to know that sitting in the back room are caskets and services for as little as $200?" A survey of 116 funeral homes in Maine found that one-third failed to display their least expensive casket.

One Washington consumer reported: "When I inquired if they did have any caskets for sale under $500, I was told, 'Oh, we have a few out in the garage that are just plain black and for use with welfare cases only. They are so dusty, you surely would not want to look at them.'" A former casket manufacturer, funeral director, and Texas state legislator noted that funeral directors tell the manufacturer to "make it look as bad as you can," and that manufacturers do produce ugly caskets which the funeral directors point to with a shrug, saying, "Well, here is our least expensive one."

These merchandising strategies have been developed into a science that is taught in some mortuary schools. Besides displaying cheap caskets in the worst light, some directors intimidate the deceased's family with comments like: "This is the last act you can perform for your mother." "He deserves better than that." "Consider what the neighbors will think when they see the casket." "Spend enough to do credit to the deceased."

Some organizations have been formed to provide people with cheap coffins. The St. Francis Burial and Counseling Society, for example, provides a pine coffin for as little as $]60 (or $]]5 for a coffin kit) plus shipping costs. The society also provides "How To Build Your Own Coffin" plans ($2.50) together with suggestions on practical uses for the coffin as a storage chest, book shelf, coffee table, wine rack, or bench until it is needed as a coffin. I must admit, using a coffin as a coffee table is a bit much, but the other suggestions are not unreasonable.

Regular caskets vary greatly in price. Sales statistics maintained by the Casket Manufacturers Association showed the following average wholesale charges in]975: cloth-covered wood, $98; steel, $224; hardwood, $300; copper or bronze, $995. These prices must be adjusted upward for inflation by approximately 8.5 percent a year. Price can also vary depending on whether the casket is "sealed," that is, supposedly watertight. But not matter how well-embalmed the body and how airtight the casket, the body will decay.

Cremation. Many Catholics are still under the false impression that their dead must be buried and not cremated. This is no longer true, although the church's "preference" is "for the custom of burying the dead in a grave or tomb." But as is explained in the introduction to the Rite of Funerals: "Christian funeral rites are permitted for those who choose to have their bodies cremated unless it is shown that they have acted for reasons contrary to Christian principle." Thus, unless the reason for choosing cremation is a disbelief in the Resurrection or some other Christian principle, cremation is permitted. The officiating priest can deal with the problem of "denial of Christian principles" or scandal or confusion by making a proclamation of belief in the Resurrection through the prayers and/or homily. And the rites ordinarily performed at the cemetery chapel or at the grave may be used in the crematory building.

Numerous people, myself included, have been told that a casket is required even if the body is going to be cremated. However, no state has an explicit casket requirement. Statutes in Maine and New Hampshire require a body to be shipped to a crematory in a casket or other suitable container. Florida law permits crematories to require "a container in the form of a cardboard container...or a wooden box or casket." Five states (California, Maryland, Minnesota, New Mexico, and Wisconsin) have specifically prohibited any requirement of a coffin.

Funeral directors will often say that a casket is required to ship the body to the crematory or that the crematory requires a casket. The Cremation Association of North America has indicated that caskets are definitely not necessary for cremation. In fact, there are many other types of containers suitable for holding and transporting a body that are available to funeral directors. Under the general heading of "alternative containers" are rigid boxes made of pressed wood, heavy cardboard or composition and opaque canvas or polyethelene pouches (such as were used in Vietnam). These containers are far less expensive than caskets, some wholesaling for as little as $5.

The cost of the cremation itself is usually between $50 and $150. Containers or urns for the ashes are priced between fifty and several hundred dollars. Final disposition costs vary with the type of disposition chosen: A niche in a columbarium can cost from $50 to $750; a burial in a cemetery may cost between $50 and $150 (less expensive than a full-sized plot); scattering can cost as much as $250 if done through a commercial service.

Sometimes a casket may be needed for services prior to cremation. Thus, families who desire public viewing of the deceased and a funeral service prior to cremation may wish to purchase a casket, but this is not always necessary. Visitation or viewing might utilize a "viewing dais" instead of a casket. A service may be held with the cremation container covered by a pall. Finally, it is also sometimes possible to rent a casket for the viewing and funeral.

F.T.C. Proposed Regulations. After a five-year study of

the funeral industry, the F.T.C. staff drafted a series of regulations in 1978 to protect consumers from unfair and anticompetitive practices by funeral home operators. These regulations were then subject to public comment and were weakened because of complaints from the funeral industry. In March of 1979, the F.T.C. met to consider the regulations, and it hopes to promulgate final rules by 1980.

The F.T.C. regulations require that funeral directors give price information over the telephone. They must also provide a written pricelist by mail or at the funeral home to anyone requesting it. The purpose of this requirement is to allow consumers to do comparative shopping.

The pricelist must disclose the retail prices of all caskets offered which do not require special ordering. In addition, the following notice must be printed on the pricelist: "1. No law requires that you buy a sealer or protective casket except in special circumstances. 2. You do not have to buy a casket if you want cremation. Caskets are listed from least expensive to most expensive. If you want to see a listed casket which is not on display, please ask."

The funeral home must also provide a pricelist for other services: embalming, transportation, use of the funeral home for services or viewing, use of hearse, limousine, etc. The funeral director must also disclose the cost (with and without his commission) of services provided by others: clergy, florist, death certificate, newspaper notices, etc.

Each customer must also be provided with a written agreement listing the services and merchandise selected by him together with the price for each item.

Consideration was given to requiring funeral homes to display in their casket selection rooms the cheapest casket they carried, but the commission feared that such a requirement would be counterproductive since some funeral homes would merely discontinue carrying the cheaper models.

The regulations do forbid requiring a casket for cremation. Also under consideration is a requirement that funeral directors who offer cremation must make available an alternative container to any consumer who desires to purchase one instead of a casket for cremation. The F.T.C. likes the idea, but it is not sure it has the legal authority to demand that merchants carry a certain type of merchandise.

The commission also forbade the embalming of a body without permission from a legally authorized family member or representative. The commission has found that embalming without permission was a not-uncommon practice. Under the proposed regulations, if the body is embalmed without approval, the family does not have to pay for the embalming.

The original regulations also forbade false or misleading statements regarding legal or religious requirements dealing with funerals. This rule was dropped but later it was restored except for the "religious" requirements. The F.T.C. felt that it was possible to police false claims about legal requirements, but it did not want to get into deciding what was or was not a false or misleading statement about religious requirements. Because of the variety of religious customs, the F.T.C. probably made an intelligent decision here. At the same time, this now leaves to churches the responsibility of policing funeral homes to make sure that they do not misrepresent religious requirements on customs like cremation.

It should be remembered that these are proposed regulations subject to approval and change by the F.T.C. The final regulations will probably not go into effect until next year.

Churches' Responsibility. That some members of the funeral industry have been able to treat the public unfairly while working with churches to bury the dead, is a disgrace. Most pastors will not give their parishioners advice about funeral services. Some do not want to appear to favor one funeral director over another. Most do not know the field themselves and, therefore, would not want to give advice on something in which they have no expertise. Others, perhaps, are influenced by the lucrative donations or advertising in the parish bulletin that come from funeral homes.

Dioceses are no better. Funeral homes advertise in the diocesan papers, which may be reluctant, as a result, to run an expose of the local funeral industry. Since churches or dioceses frequently own cemeteries, they have a conflict of interest because of their relationships with the industry. An average sized cemetery can easily net a quarter of a million dollars a year. It is not surprising, then, that although churches take positions on everything from the Panama Canal Treaty to SALT II, most have avoided the issue of regulating the funeral industry. Individual members of the clergy have been very active on both sides of the issue. The U.S. Catholic Conference did not comment. This is surprising, considering that burying the dead is a very traditional corporal work of mercy about which the church should have something to say. The National Council of Churches is in the process of preparing a position on the funeral industry.

One director of a major Catholic cemetery testified against regulatory overkill by the F.T.C. He feared that funeral practices would be hemmed with such detailed operating regulations that costs could be adversely affected. His experience over the years with funeral directors indicated that their shortcomings were hardly endemic.

After studying the final proposed regulations, he concluded, however, that "They are all reasonable as they stand now. Whether they are <u>necessary</u> is difficult to answer. Individually, some of them don't address any particular major flaw of which I am aware; collectively, as a body of rules, they address a certain historical mind set that needed to be modified. A mystique had developed around funeral service, that it was gauche if not immoral to question prices or to do any pre-shopping. Funeral directors played a part in that, but I believe some of it was built by the public itself. I have tried to look at these rules as though they had been imposed on cemeteries, but virtually all of them recommend practices that we ourselves follow, so it is difficult to find major fault with them. Probably a major irritant is a sense of stigma that attaches to having the government step in and legislate industry practices."

<u>Preparing Your Own Funeral</u>. If after reading this article you decide to prepare your own funeral, there are a number of things you should keep in mind. It is best to leave written instructions for your funeral, since that will avoid arguments among the family over what you wanted. Make sure someone knows where you have left these instructions.

The instructions should specify whether you want to be cremated or not, whether you want a casket and at what cost, whether you want to be embalmed, how much should be spent on flowers, and where your remains should be placed. Some people also wish at this time to donate their bodies or some of their organs to a hospital or medical school. If a body is accepted by a medical school, the cost for burial or cremation is, of course, eliminated. Since many medical schools have received in this way more bodies than they need, alternative plans should be made in case your body is rejected.

These decisions can have a tremendous financial effect on the family you leave behind. As the F.T.C. noted: "Funeral costs vary enormously among different funeral homes and among different kinds of dispositions and ceremonies. For example, the cost of donating a body to medical science may be only a minimal fee for transportation of the body; an immediate cremation may cost $250-$350; an immediate ground burial may cost $420-$500; a cremation after a funeral service may cost $650-$800; and a typical traditional funeral with ground burial may cost $2,200-$2,400 for both funeral and burial expenses." The sky is the limit, of course, for extras.

It is your body. Plan now, die later.

Thomas Reese

CHAPTER TWENTY-ONE

Suggested Readings

Console One Another: Guidelines for Christian Burial. A 38-page booklet compiled by priests in the Archdiocese of Milwaukee in February 1979. Deals with the liturgical rites, the place of burial, cremation, and other related questions. Available free of charge from 3257 S. Lake Drive, Milwaukee WI 53207.

A Manual of Death Education and Simple Burial by Ernest Morgan. Now in its seventh edition, this book is the manual for the Continental Association of Funeral and Memorial Societies in the United States and Canada. It deals with death education, simple burial and cremation, memorial societies, and the donation of body parts. 64 pages. Available for $2 from Suite 1100, 1828 L Street, N.W., Washington, D.C. 20036.

The Right to Die by William May and Richard Westley. Chicago: The Thomas More Press, 1980. Opposing opinions presented on the options available to people who face a life-threatening illness.

Ethical Issues Relating to Life and Death ed. John Ladd. New York: Oxford University Press, 1979.

Death By Choice by Daniel Maguire. A book describing the ethical, legal, and moral choices involved for people who are terminally ill. New York: Schocken Books, 1975.

PART VIII
Aspects of Grieving

One can never know how long it will take to work through the loss of a loved one. Each person and each relationship is unique. Only the person left behind — a spouse, a parent, a child, a brother or a sister — can know the full depth of the love and meaning that was shared over many years' time.

This section has five chapters. The first speaks about grieving in a variety of contexts. It is written by a woman whose husband died when they had six children under ten years of age. The second and third chapters contain reflections written by a widow about her own grief process, and by a college senior whose father died at the start of her first year in colleg'

CHAPTER TWENTY-TWO

Grieving

Grief is an all-consuming experience. Grief is pain, emptiness, isolation. Grief is full of the unexpected and questions without answers. There is resentment in grief, resentment of the loss. There can be resentment of the tremendous effort it takes to be in charge of yourself, or anything else for that matter.

While grief is still poorly understood, those who have studied it agree that it is a normal process, that it takes time, and that what you are thinking and feeling needs to be expressed and wept over before one will again feel healed and able to function. How long the process takes as well as its forms have some common denominators and a lot of individual differences. There are no pat solutions, but knowing what others have experienced can be both helpful and comforting.

C.S. Lewis wrote after the death of his wife, "There is a sort of invisible blanket between the world and me." Our societal structure makes mourning difficult. We are supposed to be strong. Expression of emotion in public is frowned upon. Yet the bereaved person needs support in order to face the pain of mourning and work through it.

The isolation a bereaved person experiences can be complex. Even when family and friends are available and would like to help, he or she may feel that no one is really strong enough to bear the overwhelming kind of emotions he or she is feeling. And there can be the feeling that the pain is much too immense to inflict on anyone else.

It is also true that some close friends or relatives are very uncomfortable with grief or mourning, and a bereaved person can sense this and find himself avoiding any revelation of what he is feeling or any expression of emotion. It has been expressed as being an embarrassment to people one meets as they fumble for the right thing to say.

The person who is willing to listen, and to make it known he or she is available for listening, can be a vital support to someone working through grief. This kind of person can convey to his or her friend that it is all right to cry and that it is all right to tell some of the same stories and reminiscences over and over about the loved one who is now gone.

Weeping is not all there is to mourning, but it is important. And it is also true that different losses are accompanied by different degrees of grief. In addition to tears, mourning is a process of emotional gear shifting and regrouping, as it were.

One mother of six children who lost her husband fifteen months ago said she is going through a very difficult, painful period right now. She said she feels very confused about sorting out who she is and where she is going.

She said she thinks she was so busy worrying about everybody else that she really didn't have time to think. She said that because there was so much to do during the first year after her husband died that she didn't "let the pain happen."

She finds her greatest comfort and strength in prayer and going to church, and spiritual reading has helped her too. She can see her 14-year-old son seems to be going through some of the confusion now that she is experiencing. He turns to his older brothers and uncles for support, and she is glad he is willing to do this.

Physical symptoms can be part of grief. It has been expressed as tightness in the throat or chest, loss of appetite, or emptiness in the stomach. It can be a restlessness, a searching for activity, and an inability to

concentrate. It can be forgetfulness, wandering aim-
lessly, and not finishing things. As C.S. Lewis wrote,
"And no one ever told me about the laziness of grief.
Even shaving. What does it matter now whether my
cheek is rough or smooth?"

A study was made rating a variety of human
experiences that cause stress. Called Holmes-Rahe
Social Readjustment Scale, the study rated everything
from a jail term and being fired at work to changing
jobs and retirement. Of the 44 situations rated in the
study, the death of a spouse heads the list with a score
of 100. Since stress is known to have physical effects,
the bereavement time is an important time to consider
one's own health. Being in this kind of stress makes one
more susceptible to illness and disease. The motivation
to be concerned about one's own health at this time is
very low, but it is important to eat properly, even if it is
not enjoyable, and to get adequate rest, although sleep
may be restless and is often accompanied by dreaming
of the loved one. If friends urge someone in grief to see
his or her doctor, it is wise to do so even if it doesn't
seem to make sense at the time.

As to psychological needs, many people are more
emotionally upset during bereavement than at any other
time in their lives, and they are frightened by this.
Severe upset is not unusual, but help should be sought if
it is of great concern. Making one's needs known to
those closest and most trusted will enable them to help
and give needed support. Since everyone needs help at
certain times of life, it is a distorted kind of pride that
hinders us from asking and making our needs known.
Needs may be for being alone as well as for
having someone with you. The need to have someone
around does not mean one will create a dependency that
will last forever.

Mood changes are not uncommon, and crying can come
at unexpected times. It is not uncommon to feel anger
toward the loved one for leaving. Many people feel a

sense of the loved one's presence, expecting him or her to walk in the room, or to hear the familiar voice or seeing the familiar face.

A man who lost his wife to cancer said, "Betty had written me a letter during her last months about our life together, and cautioned me against building a shrine to her in my mind. She said to remember she had faults too. But as time progresses the faults seem so trivial when matched against her strengths that my loss became more pronounced as I see the lack of these strengths in others, including myself." Forgetting the faults and remembering the good is another thing that happens during the grief process.

Guilt can be part of grief. Could something have been done differently? Things said or unsaid, missed opportunities can become distorted or exaggerated in one's mind. A grief counselor suggests that we must be more forgiving of ourselves to be at peace, concentrating more on the love that was shared than its limitations.

Personal faith is frequently a major source of comfort during bereavement. For some, however, maintaining faith may be difficult during this period of loss. Either reaction may occur, and both are consistent with later spiritual growth. When someone feels he just doesn't want to burden anyone with his sadness often finds sustenance in his belief and trust in God.

Though well-intentioned, close friends or family occasionally can add to the pain a grieving person is experiencing. A young mother who took care of her father at home during his final illness writes, "I found it painful for people to say, 'It's better that he's dead.' I would want to reply, 'It's not better, not better he got sick in the first place, not better that I no longer have him on earth, that there's nothing better to be said about the whole deal.' I knew they meant it was better he no longer had to suffer, but often that wasn't said. It came across to me as their saying it's better that my dad had died. That hurt."

Another man who lost his wife said, "People treat you like they think they would like to be treated." He found himself being rude when he was pulled into social situations before he was ready.

What is ultimately worked through in the process of grief is the gradual acceptance of the reality that a loved one is gone and will not return. It is a gradual acceptance too of how one's life has changed because of the loss and the choices that need to be made to keep moving on. It takes time to learn to live with thoughts like, "I seemed to focus on the fact that I'd lost someone I felt truly knew, accepted, and loved me just as I am and that I had that relationship with no one else. I would have thought I'd miss being with my Dad, or sharing with him, more than I'd miss an attitude of his toward me."

Friends and family are often available early in bereavement and less so later. It is important to be able to reach out to them when you need them. Don't wait for them to guess your needs. They will often guess incorrectly and too late.

During a period of grief it can be difficult to judge new relationships. Don't be afraid of them, yet it is usually wise not to rush into them. Sometimes in an effort to stop the pain of grief, people turn toward replacing the lost person (such as the adoption of a child or remarriage) too soon. It is hard, though, to see new relationships objectively if you are still actively grieving, and this kind of solution may only lead to other problems.

Most people find it best to remain settled in familiar surroundings until they can consider their future calmly. It is not wise to make major decisions within the first year unless absolutely necessary. Hasty decisions should be avoided. Seeking good advice, even from more than one person, can be helpful before making important decisions. The advice of experts is helpful before making major financial decisions.

Having a job or doing volunteer work can be helpful when one feels ready. Since a job will not fulfill all needs, it is important not to turn to excessive involvement in work. Relationships with family and friends should not be sacrificed in an effort to keep busy.

CHAPTER TWENTY-THREE

The Process of Grief For a Widow

I want to put down in writing how my husband's death affected me. It occurred six years ago, but the memory of it stays with me very clearly, and, of course, I have been shaped by it in ways I know nothing of.

I remember coming back into the house about two weeks after Ned's death, after I had waved good-bye to my sister going back to Austin. She had stayed a good ten days with me, and came back from the car twice to kiss me good-bye again. I came back into the house so alone and walked up to Ned's picture on the mantle and just said to him that nobody could help me in what I was facing except God and himself.

I am not a crying person. I think it is better if one is— things build up so tight inside oneself and find no release otherwise. I carried around an awful load of guilt because of that, and for a thousand things that had happened over our years together when I felt I had failed him in his need and been unbelievably selfish in my own. But as for getting to the place where I was human and could feel, I might as well have been made of wood.

All through the ordeal of the lawyers and the bank and the insurance companies I was afraid of proving totally inadequate, so that everything inside of me was just one deep chasm of fear. How was I going to handle all this stuff, and how was I going to find it possible to live without him?

I prayed as well as I could, feeling guilty about that too because it was so lacking. I took to spending hours reading the Bible. I had never read all the epistles before, and I kept going back to my husband through them. Ned and I always reached out to God through each other, and having to seek and find God without him was terribly trying.

Looking back, it seems as if my pain and emptiness did not last that long after all. After several months I had an experience that seemed to make it all go away. I really cannot recall the exact way it happened, but it seemed to me that a strong and very certain hand almost reached inside my body—in which there was nothing else but a close-woven mass of heavy black yarn, going up and down and across and back and forth and diagonally—the woof was Ned's and my life together, knit so close that there was no room for anything else; that hand tore out of me all I had as my life, completely, almost ruthlessly, but in love.

Then I had my Cry, finally—for all the time since the day poor Dr. Culligan had to say the word cancer to me, I had steeled myself that day to be my husband's strength and support and comfort, and I did my very utmost to be all of that. Only, and how I grieve about this for us both, when I see what hospice programs are doing to ease this cross for people—we never, either of us, put words to what our hands and eyes were saying to each other. We did have one long, beautiful good-bye, a whole morning all to ourselves, in a hospital where hardly fifteen minutes went by that someone didn't come in trying to help. I thank God so much for that still, and I had that much to begin with as I began finding my way back to him again.

I think, because Ned loves me and pestered God about me, that I was reborn that summer after he died. It's amazing how grateful I am to the many new people who began to filter into my life at that time, giving me acceptance (do not ever mention the word "resignation") and peace and much joy. I know now this is mine to keep and share.

CHAPTER TWENTY-FOUR

A Daughter's Reflections on Her Father's Death

Near the end of 1981 my family and some close friends gathered in our house to commemorate my father's death three years earlier. We felt a common bond in sharing the experience of knowing such a great human being. His laughter and care had gently touched each of us in a particular way, and we still felt lonely inside, realizing anew that we could not have him among us.

Accepting his loss remains today as the most difficult thing I have ever faced in my life. The experience has matured me, I know, but it also continues to be a part of my thoughts and outlook. Grief is a funny thing—you think you are finished with it, and then it comes back again in new and different ways.

My father was 42 when he learned he had a malignant tumor. I was away at college, 350 miles away from where I most wanted to be: at home with my dad and the rest of the family. I felt very alone at school, but my dad's encouragement to stay in school motivated me to make things work out. Looking back, I realize that his challenge was just what I needed. Otherwise, I would have dropped out of school and stopped an important aspect of my life when it was not necessary to do so. At the time my emotions were running wild. I was angry, lonely, and fearful of an uncertain future.

I do not think anyone—the doctors, my mother, my sisters, and my brother—expected that the cancer would be so destructive in such a short period of time. When we found out about the tumor in September 1978, we were frightened, but we were also hopeful that the doctors would be able to cure my father. However, in the months that followed it became evident that the cancer was spreading and that life was becoming increasingly painful for dad.

I came home for a weekend in October and noticed that he had a difficult time walking, getting in and out of the car, and maintaining his normal weight. This was the first time I had gone with him to his daily radiation treatment so I could see what his therapy entailed. It was hard for me to see my father, a person whom I had always seen as such a strong man, so helpless and dependent on others. I remember asking why a loving God would put him in such an anguishing situation. It just did not seem fair.

Dad's condition was up and down in the months of November and December. He felt good one day but on other days he would cry out in pain. He was always at home except for the week after Thanksgiving, when he spent some time in the hospital.

It was much easier for us to care for him at home because then we could continue to live our own lives as normally as possible. My sisters and brothers could come home from school and visit with dad, as against having to go down to the hospital and spend time with him in an impersonal institutional setting. I know dad really appreciated us being with him because he could still be part of the family routine. I remember times when he commented from his bed that was set up in the dining room that he wanted us to speak up more when we talked over dinner at the kitchen table. I also recall his telling me one morning that I had come in a bit late the night before. As much as I disliked the comment, I felt good that he was still able to be a father for me in this way.

One Year Later

I see many changes that have occurred for the family since my father died. Duties that he handled routinely have now become challenges for each of us: fixing a broken lawn mower, putting on a new roof, repairing faulty plumbing. They are painful reminders of his absence. I personally found it difficult when I had to go to the Social Security office to apply for benefits for myself. All of this has taken much patience, but as time passes we are managing better.

Through dad's death all of us have grown closer to each other. Mom has been a great example to us both in her strength and in her ability to express her emotions. Her faith that we will always be taken care of despite the struggles and suffering helps me not to be angry with God or fearful of the hardships we face from time to time. Because of the pain we have shared in as a family we seem to communicate more freely and deeply with one another. Maybe it's just because we're getting older, or that since Dad's bout with cancer was so brief we all realize more keenly that life is too short to take anyone or anything for granted.

Two other things stand out from my perspective of three years. I have become more sensitive and compassionate in listening to others' hardships. For example, when my roommate was grieving over a close relative's death I felt I could be supportive to her because of my own experience. Beforehand, I would have avoided such encounters in fear that I would not say or do the correct things. Also, in consequence of dad's sickness, my sister has decided to develop her gift of sensitivity by choosing a career in nursing.

Perhaps the most important changes have centered around our values. Dad's death illuminated those aspects in life that count most. No longer are we as concerned with social pressures such as keeping ahead of others on the material level; instead, we have a deeper perception about the centrality of people and relationships in life.

I still miss dad very much. I know that what we shared together continues to affect all areas of my personality and interests. His impact on me and on our family keeps us growing, in all types of situations and relationships. I feel fortunate. I feel fortunate that, despite so great a loss, I have had the help I needed to get through the past year.

Kathy Kuehl

CHAPTER TWENTY-FIVE

What Can I Say?

The death of someone we know and care about is always immensely painful, but the experience can be even more painful because of the awkwardness of not knowing what to say. Our staff has learned much from the families we have worked with, and we would like to share some of their thoughts with you.

It is most important to respect each family's unique style of coping. At one end of the continuum there are families who talk easily about their feelings and all that this loss means to them, while at the other end are those who are not expressive in this way. As a friend you might offer opportunities to talk and let the family's response be a cue to their place on this continuum.

Phrases like "It must be hard for you. What do you need. Is there any way I can be helpful?" might open doors and offer opportunities to discover both emotional and practical needs. Keep the focus on this particular family—stories of other people's illnesses and death are usually not comforting, and can be distressing. Visits to people who are seriously ill need to be brief, but the family, not wanting to discourage your interest, may find it difficult to tell you that. Your presence means as much as your words, so don't let the fear of "saying the wrong thing" keep you silent—or away altogether.

Families appreciate friends coming to the wake and the funeral. A simple embrace or handshake can speak volumes, and is more important than how you word your condolences. Written notes, especially those that share a remembrance of the person who died, are also helpful.

But the bereaved family needs more. Their time of grieving lasts many months, and they need your continued support and care throughout this period. The phrase "If you need anything, just call me" is a common one. While well-intentioned, it is often impossible for the bereaved to reach out and ask anyone for anything. Their lack of response can be misinterpreted as an indication that they want to be left alone, but usually the opposite is true—they are too lonely to even let you know.

Sometimes there are differing styles of communication within families. One woman was upset because she couldn't get her father to talk with her about his dying. Further discussion revealed he had rarely talked about personal matters throughout his 70 years, and that it was her need to let him know how much she loved him. She decided a letter might be best because then she could be certain to say what she wanted, without pressuring him to be someone he was not.

Another woman heard a talk given by one of our staff and was moved to write her mother a thank-you letter for caring for her father during his terminal illness some 15 years before. She had been a high school freshman at the time, and only as an adult could appreciate all that had been involved. Such letters are always welcome.

These are some of the things that we have learned about from families. If there are experiences that you wish to share on this topic, we would be happy to hear from you.

Kathy Dahlk, M.S.W.

CHAPTER TWENTY-SIX

Suggested Readings

A Grief Observed by C.S. Lewis. New York: Bantam Books, 1963.

A Time to Grieve: Loss As a Universal Human Experience by Bertha Simos. New York: Family Service Association of America, 1979.

The Bereaved Parent by Harriet Sarnoff-Schiff. New York: Crown Publishers, 1977.

Bereavement: Studies of Grief in Adult Life by Colin Murray Parkes. New York: Penguin Books, 1972.

PART IX
New Spiritual Images

The word "spiritual" connotes different things to each person. Most basically, it refers to the broadest questions and issues of human existence: where do we come from, what is the purpose of life, how does pain have meaning, and is there an afterlife?

Hospice as a philosophy focuses on the physical, emotional, and spiritual needs of the patient-family unit. This section highlights the delicacy of providing spiritual care to people who are dying. It is meant to apply to people of all faith backgrounds, for when a person has a short time left to live the particular issues of denominational structures and creeds take on diminished importance and concern. It is essential that no matter what the faith stance of a given family is, the freedom of choice and interest expressed by either the patient or family in the area of religion is carefully respected by all members of the hospice team.

CHAPTER TWENTY-SEVEN

Spiritual Care

Chaplains come in all shapes, denominations, sexes, and sizes. Some are particularly skilled in praying spontaneously or holding hands. Others do best when dealing with family members, rather than the patient, or in bereavement follow-up. Communion calls, reading from scripture, helping to make funeral arrangements, supporting health care professionals—these can all be part of the chaplain's role in a health care setting. But, regardless which of these a chaplain excels in, his or her work will be deficient if it is not sustained by two key ingredients: a living faith and a great capacity to listen to the needs of others.

When a family member is dying these chaplaincy skills take on a unique importance. If properly carried out, the chaplain's intervention can be a source of great support for patient and family alike; if a chaplain is half-hearted or uncertain about how and where to be present, the loss that results is a serious one. The chaplain is required to perform a delicate highwire balancing act on varying kinds of wire. She/he is expected to intervene with God for the patient and family, with petitions of hope, healing, and forgiveness. The chaplain also serves as a mediator between the patient and one or more family members who are not yet able to accept the reality of the patient's impending death.

In some situations a family will ask the chaplain to meet with a particular physician or nurse so that a misunderstanding that has occurred can be straightened out, or to help clarify the options for treatments that are available to their loved one. Most chaplains expect to assist patients in sorting out the myriad feelings of anger, disbelief, and denial that arise when surgery or chemotherapy has been unable to halt the growth of a cancerous tumor or the malfunctions of a heart.

Chaplaincy training programs have sensitized them to these expressions of struggle, along with their own personal feelings of loss and anger when confronted with these.

They are perhaps less ready to discern whose needs— those of the patient, a family member, or their own-- they are fulfilling when they enter a room to say a prayer, face a patient with his/her dying, or perform a sacramental ritual. Spouses have been known to tell a minister that a mate "wants to settle something religious with you"; however, when the minister is alone with the spouse this seems to be the last thing in the world the patient is interested in.

These issues are mentioned at the outset of this article because they form the fabric of professional chaplaincy. Anyone can do well in situations where the patient has a strong faith and is ready for death, the family is unified in acceptance and support, and the rapport with the nurses and doctors is all that it should be. At these times it is an enriching privilege to be present as a chaplain. These are, unfortunately, not the situations we spend most of our hours ministering to.

It comes down to recognizing the complexity of needs and expectations that serious illness occasions, and then knowing what role I as a limited human being can realistically carry out for a particular family.

The following pages are meant to be descriptive rather than proscriptive. They are suggestions about what to watch for with families as well as encouragement to utilize the full array of options that are available to professional chaplains.

The Appropriate Level of Response

For the most part, chaplains are not present to teach people how to die, or to bring about deathbed conversions. Their role is to assist the patient and family in the areas of need that they indicate they want help on. These may or may not be the ones that the chaplain thinks are most important; they may or may not be dealt with at the level that the chaplain feels is appropriate; but no matter. What counts is the initiative and invitation that the patient and family provide.

In this context the words "spiritual" and "religious" can be viewed in their broadest scope: ultimate concern about the value and meaning of human existence.

Whether suffering has a purpose, why someone has not been cured, the use of narcotics, the possibility of an afterlife, options about life-support systems—families discuss these issues with chaplains as well as those that involve prayer, scripture, and sacramental rituals. Death is the ultimate religious challenge precisely because it is the ultimate human challenge.

The chaplain's task is to locate and respond to the patient's need at the level where it manifests itself. If the patient is distressed because the dinner tray just came and the potatoes are lukewarm, that is something a chaplain can attend to. If a family member has not been in to visit for many days and the patient is wondering why, a chaplain can help learn why this has occurred.

A patient's fear of dying may be more related to a fear of intense pain or being left alone than to the actual moment of death. A chaplain can always be on safe ground by asking a patient to elaborate on a statement he/she has just made, or by playing back to him or her what he/she seems to be saying to ensure that it is being correctly understood. Simply being able to discuss the fear may alleviate it; or it may involve further steps by the chaplain, such as alerting the nurse that the medication is not adequately controlling the pain.

If a person is, indeed, anxious about not being ready to

meet God because of past failings or some other reason, these concerns cannot be dismissed with a hearty, "Oh, that's nothing for you to worry about." There may, in fact, be something very specific that needs discussion and possible reconciliation before a person can face death in peace. One of our hospice patients was extremely restless a short time before his death. Strong medication was not helping him at all, and we were at a loss to know what would calm him, until someone remembered that years ago he had been married outside of the church he was raised in, and that this had always distressed him. His usual chaplain had come in a few days earlier, but now a representative from the church he grew up with was contacted. He came over immediately and within a short time the man became very peaceful and able to let go of his life with great simplicity and calm.

The measure of a successful chaplaincy visit does not always lie with the content of the exchange or the explicitness of the religious language used. What counts is the effort made to listen to and support the patient at the level that she/he chooses to be engaged at this particular time. As John Swift writes in an article entitled "Meeting Spiritual Needs":

"The Chaplain can distinguish a disparity between verbal content—'God is in heaven and all is well in creation'—and experienced religious concerns—'I'm scared, alone, abandoned, guilty.' A very religious pastoral call may never include mention of God, Jesus, Moses, the Bible, or prayer." Manual of the Royal Victoria Hospital Hospice, p. 245)

Those of us who see many sick people on a daily basis need to be reminded how serious a crisis a hospital stay, particularly one that involves impending death, can be. These patients are gradually losing control over all areas of endeavor: walking about on their own, eating, getting dressed, planning their day, bowel and bladder functions. Whether at home or in a hospital, they have a variety of telephone calls and visitors to contend with. They are generally taking strong narcotics every three to four hours and having difficulty sleeping through the night.

In this context it is no surprise that they are unable to always be polite, smiling, or "appropriately responsive" when a minister, priest, or rabbi comes for a visit. Too many earlier visitors may have worn them out; an argument with a nurse or spouse may have reduced them to tears. I have often considered sitting outside of a dying patient's room in a hospital for an entire day, merely to note down the number of people who enter the room and how long they remain there. Hospitals would do well by all of their patients if they kept some type of sign-in sheet next to a patient's door, so that both health care staff members and family visitors could have some sense of the number of people who have spent time with the patient before their arrival.

These factors are highlighted because they help explain why a chaplain must tread cautiously when entering into discussion with a patient. Usually the fact and the timing of the visit arise from the initiative of the chaplain, not the patient. In the hospital setting, all it takes is a knock on the door and the chaplain is in the room; at home such visits are generally preceded by a phone call, but even then few patients or families feel free enough to say, "No, this is not a good time for you to come and visit."

Oftentimes people do welcome a visit by a chaplain, especially if she/he is known to them or at least comes from their particular denomination. However, this may not be the particular time—or person—that a patient chooses to share some area of concern with. At the end of my first visit with patients I make it a point to mention that the next time I come they may be tired or not want another visitor. If that is the case, I encourage them to tell me this, wave their arms, do whatever is necessary to alert me to this fact, so that I can

withdraw without having my feelings hurt—thereby ensuring their comfort rather than mine. This helps, to a
point; but beyond alerting the patient, it serves as a
reminder to myself that I come into their room as an
uninvited guest.

Moving Forward Slowly

I visited one man at home regularly for a period of six
months. He knew he was dying and completed practical
details such as drawing up a will and settling his funeral
arrangements during this time. Religion was not a
matter of interest to him, but towards the last few
months he began to wonder about the possibility of an
afterlife. At one point I made a comment about what it
must have been like for Lazarus to return after being
raised from the dead, but he had never heard of the
story. I gave him Raymond Moody's book Life After
Life and the resurrection accounts from the Christian
scriptures. We discussed them several times, but it was
not until our final visit together that I felt it was
appropriate to ask him if he wanted me to say a prayer
and give him my blessing.

He said he did. After I left he said to his wife, a
Protestant, with a smile, "I think I just got the Catholic
last rites." The next night, shortly before he died, he
asked his wife to bring their two daughters, 7 and 10,
into his room for their night prayers. As they finished
his wife asked him if he felt God was close to him, and
he said, "Yes, He's right here beside me on the bed."

This example indicates how necessary it is to journey
with a patient at the pace that he/she sets. A chaplain
can be well versed in the stages of denial, anger,
bargaining, depression, and acceptance; a chaplain can
hope that when the end comes a patient has been able
to complete all necessary duties and relationships, and
is peaceful about what lies ahead. But the chaplain
must always check to ensure that these are goals the

patient is intent on achieving as well. The above example can be counterbalanced by other situations where a patient expressed no interest in receiving a blessing, discussing the possibility of an afterlife, or having scripture read to him or her.

I have visited some families at Children's Hospital regularly for weeks, without once engaging them in discussion about anything more significant than how things were going, the weather, and the local sporting scene. But then, during an evening visit when it was obvious that their daughter had a short time to live, their fears and anxieties all came tumbling out in the course of a walk up and down the hospital corridor. They covered everything, went through all stages that have ever been described, at no prodding or initiative of my own. We are not present to teach people how to die, but to support them in the ways and times that they—and their family members—choose.

Refashioning One's Image of God

The crisis of impending death—whether for oneself or someone dear to us—calls into question all the categories that people have established during the previous years of life. Words such as "hope, strength, patience, belief" take on vastly different meanings and dimensions in this context.

As people grow up, marry, and settle into their occupations they become accustomed to a great deal of independence and self-sufficiency. This is what has enabled them to survive, to manage their money, provide for their children, learn to resolve the differences in their marriage. Various illnesses crop up among the family, from colds to major surgery, but, with the help of modern medication and competent physicians, these become temporary setbacks that soon become part of the family's history. One's faith in God, prayer, and affiliation with one or other religious denomination is part of this overall pattern of meaning, achievement,

achievement, and struggle.

An impending death in the family calls into question all of these patterns of behavior and belief. The physician's skills, the hope that was provided by drugs and treatments, the opportunity to complete further dreams, the growth that came through belief in God and regular hard work—all these are dashed by the realization that time is running out, for me, for someone I love. Nothing counts, nothing matters— money, one's body, one's faith—as it did in the previous months and years before this disease began to wreak its havoc.

In Genesis God commissioned Adam and Eve to take charge of the earth: God said, "Let us make men in our own image, in the likeness of ourselves, and let them be masters of the fish of the sea, the birds of heaven, the cattle, all the wild beasts, and all the reptiles that crawl on the earth. God blessed them, saying, 'Be fruitful, multiply, fill the earth and conquer it. Be masters of the fish of the sea, the birds of heaven and all living animals on the earth.' God said, 'See, I give you all the seed-bearing plants that are upon the whole earth, and all the trees with seed-bearing fruit; this shall be your food." (Genesis]:26-28, The Jerusalem Bible)

That passage has served as a mandate for all human beings raised in the Judaeo-Christian tradition to go forth and develop the earth, to use their intelligence and free will to the utmost capacity that they are capable of. But when the end time comes for people on this earth, they oftentimes doubt whether they understood God's message from the beginning. "Why is He doing this to me now? How can He ask this of our family?"

Death is always a difficult mystery to face. Frequently the situation is compounded because the illness occurs just when a couple is beginning to enjoy their retirement, or before they have had the opportunity to experience the fruits of the years spent in raising a family. No matter what the particular circumstances, the sting of death is that you know that this particular person—be it a spouse, a parent, a child—will never again be there by your side to share in the joy and challenge of life with you. And he, in his illness, must cope with the loss of everything: bodily functions, friends, career, life itself.

Spouses who have shared a few or many years together experience the full impact of their vow formula in this context:

"I, _____, promise you, _____ to be your lawful wedded spouse. To have and to hold, from this day on in riches and poverty, in good times and bad, in sickness and in health, until death do us part."

Anniversaries, holidays, gifts that have been given or need to be bought—each of these is a further reminder that time is running out on the pattern of life together that has been established over many decades. A sensitive chaplain will appreciate the pain these losses entail for each particular family, along with the fearsome things that are occurring in the dying person's body week by week.

Death asks a person to do the opposite of God's commission in Genesis: to let go, to cease growing, controlling, asserting oneself. All the skills and efforts that were formerly needed to establish a marriage, a home, a career are now useless. In fact, they often stand in the way of facing and coping with one's own brief time that is remaining on this earth.

A chaplain can help patients and families to sort out this tumult of emotions and changing values. She/he can assist them in seeing how much they have worked through together in past years, and how God has supported them amid previous hardships and crises.

Negative images of God as an angry parent or a punitive judge may surface and need discussion. Doubts about the strength of one's faith or efficacy of one's prayer can be dealt with in the context of scripture passages describing how people such as Abraham, Jesus, Moses, and Paul faced critical periods in their own lives, and came through them because of the help received from God.

Many family members will find this a time of great challenge to their belief systems. They need encouragement that this is normal, that it takes time, and that they will receive the help they need to see it through. For some the growth and clarity will be achieved in a matter of weeks and months; others may begin a time of questioning and doubt that will last over many years, and include a period of withdrawal from all church activities and rituals. Chaplains can assist both groups of people by their accessibility, their calm, and their willingness to let God be the one who is most concerned about revealing himself to them at this time.

Lovely things can, potentially, occur in families amid the crisis of an impending death. Couples who have been distant can become closer and more loving; parents and adult children who have been estranged are sometimes able to heal their differences before the end comes. A son or daughter who could never speak openly with a parent may bridge this gap through the closeness that occurs when giving direct physical care to someone. Families can be encouraged to spend quality time together in the months when the patient is doing well, so that when the patient begins to sleep more and lose some mental and physical abilities they will not have feelings of regret for not being present enough before the death occurred.

Everyone wants to be with the patient when the death occurs, but it is not always possible, or practical. This should be discussed with families beforehand, so that if it does occur it will not cause undue pain. In the home setting it is always feasible to move slowly after the person has died, so that all family members who wish are able to come and grieve together while the body is still present. This may take several hours, but it is entirely at the family's discretion to decide when it is appropriate to call the funeral director to come for the body. This is also possible in a hospital setting, provided that the family makes this known to the nursing staff.

The chaplain is a source of support to patients and families through her/his presence, helpful suggestions, and as a person of faith and hope. For believing families, a representative of the church or synagogue has been with them at the beginning of life, during central periods of change such as confirmation, engagement, and marriage, and remains present to them now in the face of sickness and death. This speaks for itself, oftentimes without words. The chaplain, more than the nurse, the physician, or the social worker, has a role that is undefined, that touches all phases of concern and all levels of a family's need. It can sometimes be an ambiguous or awkward role, depending on the circumstances, but if one is patient and willing to learn from each family's situation, it can enrich both the chaplain and the families he/she is called to serve.

One final aspect needs to be mentioned, namely, the person of the chaplain. There is an old saying in the Christian tradition that "grace builds on nature." This is very obviously so in the context of chaplaincy work with the terminally ill. God makes use of who we are to reach out and touch the fears and pains of those who are dying. And the "who we are" is part and parcel of how the healing and hope occur.

When we are uncertain what to say in a difficult situation, there is nothing wrong with admitting that, or remaining silent altogether. Oftentimes an expression of wonder or doubt by a chaplain can be the entry into an honest discussion with a patient. If a particular person—patient or family member—is a source of anger or challenge for us, it is helpful to recognize this and, when possible, withdraw from the context or do what we can to alter it.

There is an increased emphasis today on team ministry. It is particularly helpful in working with those who are dying because it enables any member of the team—nurse, social worker, physician, chaplain—to have input into the physical, emotional, and spiritual needs of the patient and family unit. Roles frequently blur, so that a nurse may be the person asked to pray with a patient or discuss doubts of faith, things that the patient may not choose to do with the chaplain. This alleviates the burden that was formerly placed on chaplains: they were the ones responsible for all matters spiritual; they had to stick it out with a particular family even if there were serious personality conflicts that impeded positive growth and interaction between them.

The chaplain's own faith will obviously be tested amid these circumstances. As he/she recognizes this in others as a source of potential growth and deepening, so too can it be for him/herself as well. It is good for us to be pushed back to our knees, to the scriptures, to the patience and immensity that God has shown forth to humankind from the beginning of time. We must be willing to recognize our own limitations, to have people that we can rely on for hope and sustenance. And we need to take the opportunities that present themselves for our own healing, recreation, and renewal.

Practical Suggestions

If you enter a home or hospital room thinking you know what is likely to occur while you're there, you are not being open to the grace of God and the vagaries of the human situation. Knowledge about medications, life-support systems being turned on or off, hospital structures and politics—all these are necessary elements in a chaplain's survival kit.

Some words and phrases convey positive expressions of care and concern, while others inevitably turn people off. "I know what you are feeling. It's all part of God's will. He's better off now."—these fall in the latter category and should rarely be used. Some families have numerous nonverbal ways of communicating; others need to be encouraged to speak out or show their affection more directly. Families that have developed a tradition to always have someone present when a loved one is in a hospital or is nearing death are to be commended. And chaplains need to be reminded that there is usually more than one patient when a loved one is dying.

If a family member expresses concern about funeral arrangements, this should be recognized as his or her way of accepting the impending death. As difficult as it is to go to a funeral parlor and make these arrangements before the patient has died, it is twice as hard after the death has occurred. Chaplains can provide much solace and practical help to families by offering to accompany them on this difficult venture. Families who discuss the possibility of a group portrait earlier in the illness or the option of donating body parts to science need encouragement to complete these details as soon as they can, before it is too late. In all of these, a chaplain may have strong personal views and principles. They need not be imposed on families or patients, but can be expressed in a balanced way that will assist families to choose the option they are most comfortable with.

This is also true for other health care professionals who are asked by patients their views of God or the afterlife. This can best be handled by referring the question back to the patients, to see if they are interested in elaborating on their own ideas on these themes. It is not crucial that a staff member explains all that he/she does or does not believe in, but that the patient has the opportunity to say all that she/he wishes. If the question is raised a second time of the staff member, he/she should not hesitate to share their views with the patient.

Making Bereavement Visits

This is an area that receives far less attention than it deserves, particularly from chaplains. It can be as significant an involvement for chaplains as that which occurs at the time of the patient's death. Many people are present shortly before and after the death; few continue to call and stop by in the following months. And yet this is the time of maximum need and readjustment in families. The memories of the pain and suffering that were experienced begin to fade with time, but then comes the sense of emptiness and void that cries out for purpose and healing.

Other sections of this book contain background information on what grieving entails. I wish only to emphasize here the uniqueness of each particular loss in a family. No two marriages are alike. No two relationships between parents and children or brothers and sisters are alike. When a child dies before the parent does, a part of one's life, one's biology, has been destroyed, no matter if the loss occurs when the parent is 22 or 95. The time it will take to reintegrate one's life and move forward in a constructive way is two to three times as long as may be expected when an elderly parent or grandparent dies.

Many people are uncomfortable with crying in front of others, particularly in front of ministers and priests. Many chaplains are uncomfortable with people crying in front of them. As Cicely Saunders says, "What counts is what you allow individuals to tell and share with you." A man in his forties, on expressing embarrassment over his tears, can be gently reminded that this is not something he should be ashamed of, but rather something he should be proud of because it expresses the love and intimacy that were developed and enjoyed over many years of marriage.

A teenage daughter, wondering about how to share her memories of her mother when the first anniversary of the death arrives, can be encouraged to write a letter to her father that relates some of the good times they all shared in as a family. Even the "thank-you" notes sent after a funeral has been completed can be a source of comfort for both family members and friends alike, if they are written with care and directness:

"Your expression of sympathy for the family of Marshall Bruce is greatly appreciated. We have found much consolation from these kindnesses. Our hope is that you who knew him will also be consoled by our reminding you that as a man who truly celebrated life, Marshall cherished his friends. He considered being of use to another his foremost reason for living, his greatest joy. So your degree of loss is probably a measure of the joy he derived from you. Enjoy your memories and offer an alleluia that your friend and our father has found eternal happiness in the friendship of God."

The degree of loss experienced is always a measure of the love that was shared and experienced. This cannot be expressed often enough to widows, widowers, parents, brothers and sisters, sons and daughters. And the length of the grieving will frequently be in direct proportion to the depth of the relationship that had developed over the decades.

Chaplains, particularly those who are not married, must be willing to give grieving spouses ample time to express the full weight of their pain. For many it is the first time they have truly been alone in their adult lives. Through their marriage they formed a unit: they went everywhere together; they shared in decision-making and lovemaking; oftentimes each could complete the other's sentence. How can a spouse become whole again, in a few short months or even years, when he/she continues to encounter situations where the extent of the loss is highlighted: getting the car fixed, filling out the tax forms, going to work, washing the clothes, spending an evening or a weekend alone?

Some spouses are so busy keeping the household running and holding down a job that they have little time to grieve in the early months after the death. The immediacy of shopping, picking up children, settling insurance claims overtakes all other considerations. But when the bottom falls out and all their defenses are down, then the need for someone to relate to is all the greater.

The greatest fear that people express at this time is that they are losing their minds. If there is someone close to them in the family to share this with, the pain can be borne. Sometimes, this is not possible. Take, for example, a woman who remarried within eight months after the death of her first husband. When she found herself at home crying over memories of her first marriage, she was unable to admit this to her present spouse, but was still in great need of talking about it with someone, be it another family member, a clergy-person, or whoever. This can also occur with parents who have lost a child. One spouse may deal with the grief without many tears or other outward expressions of sadness, while the other parent will be more directly expressive. Each wishes to protect the other from pain, and this can prevent honest sharing of need at a crucial time. A chaplain who worked with the couple during the child's illness can also be a source of strength and help during this additional crisis months later.

The situations that a chaplain encounters, both during the time of illness and in the bereavement period, are at the heart of human existence. If she/he stays with them all the way through, they can be a source of much enrichment and hope as well. Yes, on occasion, the struggle and depression are large; yes, one does become involved in many sad situations of pain and loss. But they are greatly offset by sharing with people at a critical juncture of life. You are welcomed into their homes and their hearts. You witness on a daily basis gestures of love and forgiveness that you may not see on more than a few occasions outside of this context in a year's time. People are grateful that you were there, that you cared, that you continued to keep in touch with them months later.

We do not, ever, know the full extent of God's ways and God's sense of timing. But we can share with people our own limited experiences of that loving presence, even in the face of death. Two scriptural passages, one from the Hebrew scripture, the other from the end of Matthew's Gospel, express this possibility and hope, for me, and through me to the patients and families I encounter:

> I know the plans I have in mind for you, plans for peace and not disaster reserving a future full of hope for you. When you seek me, you will find me. When you seek me with all my heart, I will let myself be found by you. It is Yahweh who speaks.

> Meanwhile the eleven disciples set out for Galilee, to the mountain where Jesus had arranged to meet them. When they saw him they fell down before him, though some hesitated. Jesus came up and spoke to them. He said, "All authority in heaven and on earth has been given to me. Go, therefore, make disciples of all nations; baptise them in the name of the Father and of the Son and of the Holy Spirit, and teach them to observe all the commands I gave you. And know that I am with you always; yes, even to the end of time."

(Scripture quotations are from The Jerusalem Bible. Garden City, N.Y.: Doubleday and Company, 1971.)

CHAPTER TWENTY-EIGHT

"L'Chaim—To Life"

A neighbor who had cared for one of our patients came
across a note the woman had written shortly before she
died. It said:
>Remember me with smiles and laughter
>Because that's how I shall remember you.
>If you can only remember me with tears,
>Don't remember me at all.

The direct, gentle tone of her words is both an
admonishment and a promise. It is difficult to imagine
what it is like to be remembered with smiles and
laughter, from the other side of death. How far can
memory reach, how much can love overcome?

The various feasts and celebrations of December are an
effort to deal with these same questions. As a Christian
I view the scripture accounts of shepherds and angels,
stars, and wise men on camels as expressions of a basic
truth: there is something, Someone, greater than all
that we see and are as human beings. Someone who can
overcome death itself.

Jewish people begin their celebration of Hanukkah this
year on the night of December 20th, the shortest day of
the year. For eight days they light candles and pray in
celebration of their freedom from King Antiochus IV in
]65 before the common era. It is a simple, joyous ritual,
but one that heightens their awareness that light is
more powerful than darkness, freedom of worship more
valuable than all other goods.

Arabs have a proverb that says, "Allah watches over the
tiny ant, under the immense rock, in the dark night." In
using these examples I am also conscious of those who
do not espouse a particular religious faith or an outlook

that includes an afterlife. But for all of us, Jew or Christian, believer or non-believer, this is a season of spirit and love. Our family rituals will vary and the motivations behind them will differ, but one thing is clear: the spirit of love is felt more deeply during this season than at any other time of year.

We all desire to be loving, to be someone for someone. In the lighting of candles and the giving of gifts amidst the heart of winter may we continue to be bound together as families who do remember, with smiles and laughter, with thanks and hope.

James M. Ewens

CHAPTER TWENTY-NINE

Suggested Readings

Living Your Dying by Stanley Keleman. New York: Random House, 1974.

Ministry To The Hospitalized by Gerald Niklas and Charlotte Stefanics. New York: Paulist Press, 1975.

Quest: The Life of Elisabeth Kubler-Ross by Derek Gill. New York: Ballantine Books, 1980.

Good Grief by Granger Westberg. Philadelphia: Fortress Press, 1971.

When Children Ask About God by Harold Kushner. New York: Schocken Books, 1976.

PART X
How to Begin a Hospice

As of January 1982, there are over 800 operative hospice programs in North America. Most of them follow the home care model first established in New Haven, Connecticut by Hospice of Connecticut in 1974. Others have first provided care within a unit of a general hospital and then broadened to include home care services as well.

The National Hospice Organization came into being in 1978, in response to the many groups of people across the country who needed help on beginning programs in their communities. The following brochure was written by the staff of the N.H.O. to assist new groups with their development plans. A wide range of other types of material are also available to those who are interested from the N.H.O. office in McLean, Virginia.

CHAPTER THIRTY

Information For Hospices

Why Are Hospices Established and By Whom?

Hospices are formed for various reasons, such as: (1) someone in the community heard or read about St. Christopher's Hospice in England, visited it, and came back enthused and then formed a group to develop a hospice in that community; (2) a nurse or a physician in a community hospital saw the need for special care for the dying patients, had read about hospices, started making inquiries and formed a hospice group; or (3) community leaders and volunteers heard about the hospice concept or saw a hospice program on TV, became interested and invited hospice people to come talk to them about it, and then worked to form a hospice.

There are now more than 800 hospice groups in the U.S. Each one of these was formed because someone with leadership qualities galvanized the community into action and formed the hospice that suited the needs of that particular community. Among those who start hospices are physicians, nurses, social workers, clergymen, and community leaders.

Needs in the community that facilitate creation of a hospice are the same everywhere. Dying people have special needs and existing health care services (i.e., acute care hospitals, nursing homes, and even some home care programs) do not adequately meet these needs.

Who perceives these needs? Sometimes it is health professionals who are involved in the care of the sick, or family members who have experienced the painful death of a loved one, or community leaders, or a group of individuals who are aware of unmet needs.

Who Funds the Establishment
and Operation of Hospices?

The hospices now in existence in the U.S. have developed their programs, including funding sources, out of their own initiatives. Hospice programs funded by Department of Health and Human Services through the National Cancer Institute (NCI) are:

a. Hospice, Inc. of New Haven, Connecticut (now Connecticut Hospice, Inc.), which was funded as a Hospice Home Care Program for three years beginning in 1973;

b. Three hospice demonstration projects were chosen out of the responders to an RFP (Request for Proposal) issued by NCI in 1977: (1) Riverside Hospice in Boonton, New Jersey (a free-standing facility); (2) Hillhaven Foundation in Tucson, Arizona (a nursing home); and (3) Kaiser-Permanente Hospital in California (a hospital-based hospice).

Aside from these federally funded programs, hospices seek funds either from private, voluntary contributions, or as grants from private foundations.

In September 1979, DHEW (as it was called then), through the Health Care Financing Administration, designated 26 already existing hospice programs as demonstration projects for Medicare and Medicaid patients. Health Care Financing Administration (HCFA) will pay for hospice care for a period of three years through these demonstration projects.

Are Funding Agencies Usually
the Initiators of Hospice Programs?

What Type of Role Do They Play in
Organizing and/or Operating a Hospice Program?

Funding sources are not usually initiators. Hospices are

first organized and then approach the funding organizations or raise money to develop their programs. This pattern is understandable because staff work is needed to write grant proposals. Also, funding agencies usually prefer to give money to programs that have shown potential for growth or demonstrated some degree of credibility.

The role of funding agencies or organizations depends on the type of funds for which the hospice program applies. These funds may either be restricted (such as funds for construction or equipment, or funds for specific purposes such as education, training, etc., and are therefore not useable for purposes other than those specified) or unrestricted. The latter are funds which may be used for any purpose, such as operating expenses, patient care, etc. Most private funding organizations give funds without requiring a say in the policies of the hospice, but they expect good progress reports and quality performance. United Way, for example, will entertain requests for funds only from programs which meet the criteria of Medicare.

The federal government usually defines client populations and examines policies, program goals, and objectives that must conform to specific guidelines before funds can be granted. For both government and private funding institutions, there are detailed instructions as to their requirements. Information pamphlets are available in most public and private libraries.

What Type of Personnel Do Hospices Utilize?

Personnel roles are usually similar to those found in most health care programs. Hospice is different from conventional health care only in the sense that the goal of hospice care is not to save the patient's life nor to prolong the life, but to make the patient as comfortable as possible and to help him to enjoy maximum quality of life within the limitations of the illness. This goal makes it necessary to include both the patient and family members in the unit of care and to have a multidisciplinary team which is capable of addressing all the needs of the dying patient and the family—i.e., physical, social, pyschologicial, and spiritual.

These characteristics of hospice care, in a way, define the roles of the members of the hospice staff. One difference is the fact that in hospices there is a blurring of roles among the personnel. Because teamwork is the basis of good hospice care, all the members of the team provide input into the various aspects of developing goals, objectives, and policies. Screening is a function of the specific department involved—i.e., the physicians are screened by the medical director, the nurses by the director of nursing, etc., with the help of the administrative division.

What Legislative and Insurance Problems Are Usually Encountered by Hospice Programs?

Legislative and insurance problems are many because the hospice concept is new in the U.S. There are rules and regulations that govern hospitals, nursing homes, and home care agencies which do not apply to hospice care. Efforts are being exerted by many hospices in several states and by the National Hospice Organization to develop legislation, standards, and criteria governing hospice care.

Several insurance carriers such as Blue Cross/Blue Shield are funding pilot projects on hospice care so that insurance problems can be solved and new policies formulated. It is a long and difficult process, but in time the problems should be satisfactorily resolved.

What Are The Most Frequently Encountered Obstacles in the Development and Operation of a Hospice Program?

Most of the obstacles are in the lack of funds to initiate a program. Once the program is started, the problems are in the reimbursement mechanisms because insurance providers usually do not cover hospice care. If patients cannot pay for their care and if insurance providers will not pay, staff cannot be paid and the program cannot continue to operate.

Who deals with these obstacles? In the absence of established procedures and official bodies which hospices can resort to, it is the individual hospices which have had to deal with these obstacles so far. The problems differ from community to community and from state to state, and this is the reason why hospices have so many different ??? Each group responds to its own needs and its own problems.

What Type of Postgraduate Training in Hospice Work Is Now Available in the U.S.?

The hospice movement came to the United States from England, and it grew so fast that neither the government's regulatory agencies nor the academic communities were quite prepared for it. Two institutions offer good courses on hospices, but they are non-degree courses. These are:

Hospice of Marin
77 Mark Drive, #6
San Rafael, California 94903
(415) 472-7490

Hospice of Connecticut, Inc.
61 Burban Drive
Branford, Connecticut 06405
(203) 789-1509

Are There Job or Career Opportunities in the Hospice Field at Present?

For someone who is thinking of a new career in hospice, it seems that being in the field of nursing or social work would be more marketable than being a counselor. However, a master's degree in nursing or an M.S.W. on top of a counseling degree could make one more qualified than others. Consideration might also be given to taking training in actual hospice work in either of the two institutions previously mentioned.

Hospice of Northern Virginia is a very good model of a hospice. Its paid staff at present consists of the following personnel:

Executive Director (M.P.H.), 100%
Executive Secretary, 100%
Home Care Coordinator (R.N.), 100%
Home Care Assistant (B.S.), 100%
Education Coordinator (M.Ed.), 50%
Volunteer Coordinator (M.N.), 50%
Social Worker (M.S.W.), 50%
Medical Director (M.D.), 50%
Hospice Staff Physician (M.D.), 35%
Clergy Volunteers

This hospice served 200 patients in its Home Care Program in a period of 30 months. The listing above will give you an idea of what jobs might be available in similar hospice programs. The counseling of families and patients is done by the M.D.'s or the R.N.'s or the S.W.'s and the clergy—all acting as a team.

What Are The Basic Steps Involved in Establishing a Hospice?

Establishment of an independent facility should not be a main goal. Hospice care is preferably given in the patient's own home whenever possible. When in-patient care is needed, some beds in an already existing community hospital can be utilized. Many operational hospice programs have taken this approach.

Once the hospice is incorporated and its board of directors organized, it can plan on developing a hospice home care program. This can be done by:

1. Applying for a certificate of need with the local health systems agency; or
2. Entering into a contract with an already-certified home health agency in the area, such as the Visiting Nurse Association or the Public Health Service.

The latter approach is easier and faster because the Visiting Nurse Association can deliver hospice care in the patient's own home and they can usually collect from insurance providers, both government and private. It is essential, however, to have a medical director even on a part-time basis, who can make house calls and be the leader of the multidisciplinary team. Some hospice groups have started by paying a physician $5,000 a year to compensate for meeting time and time on the telephone. In most states, the physician charges insurance providers for the house call ($50 in Virginia) which will provide the additional income to make hospice work feasible for him or her.

Roughly speaking, the steps that initially need to be taken are:

1. Incorporate as a nonprofit organization and work for tax-exempt status (any lawyer can help with this). Usually five incorporators are needed.
2. Elect a president, secretary, and treasurer.
3. Form a board of directors.
4. Develop a set of by-laws.
5. Raise funds to hire a core staff, even if on a part-time basis. This should include:
a. An executive director
b. A secretary

c. A medical director (M.D.) and
d. A home care coordinator (R.N.).
6. Develop a plan for a hospice home care program. Once this is underway it will provide a vehicle for voluntary contributions in the form of memorials and tax-free donations.
7. Work with an existing community hospital for the use of some beds if inpatient care is needed. Some communities have found it more practical NOT to call these beds "hospice beds" because insurance providers will pay for a regular hospitalization, but not for hospice care.
8. Use volunteers for office work at the beginning. However, having an office is important because people will call and they need an address to send donations to.

If a Building Is Available, How Can It Be Converted Into A Hospice Facility?

Starting a "hospice facility" in the United States is not as easy as it seems because it is not just a question of having a building or a home that can be converted into a hospice, but it involves complying with all the federal, state, and local regulations, policies, etc., that govern the establishment of a health care facility— which a hospice is. This means having to go to the health systems agency of the state and applying for a certificate of need for hospice beds. (This is a long process which includes public hearings, testimonials, etc.). After the certificate is granted, then applications for licensure have to be filed with the state and/or the county so that the hospice home can be operated as a facility.

The National Hospice Organization has defined hospice as a concept of care which includes both home care and inpatient care. The "hospice facility" should be part of a program of care which also includes a good hospice home care program. The hospice facility would then be the back-up for those patients on home care who can no longer be cared for at home.

A good way of starting is to approach an already certified home health care agency in the community, such as the Visiting Nurse Association or even the Public Health Service of a county, and work together on the development of a hospice program of care. They could provide the home care program and plans for the inpatient facility can be subsequently developed, if needed.

What Is Required and Expected of the Hospice Facilities?

Hospice facilities are subject to all the regulations, federal, state, and local, that govern any other health facility, be it an acute care hospital or a nursing home. Since the hospice concept of care is new in the United States, our health care system still does not have specific regulations or standards which could be used as guidelines. However, the National Hospice Organization has developed a document entitled "Standards of a Hospice Program of Care" which is available at a cost of $20. Many hospice groups in various states have also been working with their local legislatures and state departments of health on licensure requirements for hospices.

Is There a Low-Interest Government Loan Available to Renovate for Hospice Usage and Expansion?

It is doubtful if there are any available at this point in time. Hospice is too new, and the federal government is still trying to find out what its role should be, if any, in hospice care. Everything about hospice and the government is still in the process of evolution, and funds for funds for construction are therefore part of what needs to be studied much later on.

Where Can I Get a Desired or Preferred Plan For a Hospice Facility?

The National Hospice Organization does not have a desired or preferred plan for hospice facilities because each hospice designs its own plan that will serve its objectives and conform to the resources that are available to it. Once the standards and accreditation guidelines are formalized and the licensure regulations for hospices adopted, it may be easier to define what an ideal plan for a hospice facility will be like. Until that time comes, it might be easier for a new hospice group to develop its plans in cooperation with the state and county regulating agencies.

What Are the Rules and Regulations Governing the Establishment of Hospices in the U.S.?

There are as yet no rules and regulations for establishing and maintaining a hospice because hospices in various states of the U.S. are developing according to the needs and the circumstances that are unique to each individual community. Each state is also in the process of developing its own licensing requirements in order to meet the needs of hospices that are being formed. The reason for this lack of specifics is that both federal and state governments have not had time to develop policies and regulations.

Do Occupational Therapists Have a Role in Hospice Care?

"Hospice care" means making the dying as comfortable as possible and maximizing the quality of life that is remaining to the dying, either at home or in a hospice facility. This means helping the person overcome many of the limitations caused by the illness, such as self-feeding, getting out of bed, getting dressed, etc. All of these are roles for the occupational therapist.

One of the greatest problems of the dying is the boredom that comes out of not doing anything. Occupational therapists are in a unique position to devise all kinds of distractions for patients, such as basket-weaving, woodcarving, etc.

Reprinted with permission from National Hospice Organization, 1311 A, Dolly Madison Boulevard, McLean, Virginia 22101.

CHAPTER THIRTY-ONE

A Doctor and Hospice

Nine years ago, Josefina Magno discovered she had breast cancer. She had a mastectomy.

But what is a traumatic event for many became a turning point for this highly determined woman, a turning point that eventually led her to establish a hospice for the care of the dying.

Now executive director of the National Hospice Organization, Magno was interviewed Monday after arriving in Milwaukee to visit hospice programs here at the invitation of the Hospice Council of Southeastern Wisconsin.

At the time of her mastectomy, Magno, a widow and mother of seven, was a physician with the George Washington University medical department in Washington, D.C.

"The mastectomy didn't bother me," she said with a wave of her hand. "I was very peaceful about it." She opted not to have chemotherapy, but her children talked her into taking a course of radiation therapy.

It was while she was taking radiation therapy and meeting other patients in the waiting room that Magno became aware of what it meant to be a cancer patient. She decided to use her medical skills in cancer treatment.

When Georgetown University Hospital opened its division of medical oncology, she became one of the first four physicians to train as an oncologist, or cancer specialist.

Magno saw that what hospitals were doing for cancer patients wasn't enough. The experience of one patient in particular struck her. He was a man of about 55 who was in great pain with cancer. While he was hospitalized, the pain was brought under control. He went home—but then he was back again in the hospital emergency room in a few days, again in great pain.

The man's wife asked Magno to put him in the hospital again, but because no more treatment was indicated, he wasn't really eligible for hospital care. A nursing home wouldn't take him because his health insurance wouldn't cover nursing home care.

His predicament infuriated Magno. It was another turning point for her.

"I thought, 'My God, this is the richest country in the world, this man has been paying for insurance all his life, and there is nowhere for him to go. Here we were doing all kinds of sophisticated research into cancer, but when a patient reached a point in an illness we couldn't do anything," she said.

The answer, Magno knew, was an alternative form of care for terminally ill patients, the hospice. England was leading the way in the hospice movement.

"So the first chance I had, I went to England, to visit the St. Christopher Hospice. I also visited the St. Joseph Hospice there and St. Luke's," said Magno.

"I went back to Georgetown. I knew we could do anything they do in England, but the problem was the health insurance."

Magno went to the area Blue Cross-Blue Shield office and talked the insurance carrier into a hospice pilot project. She used the bottom line—cost effectiveness—as her most convincing argument.

The average cancer patient in this country spends about $23,000 over two years, Magno said. She proved to Blue Cross-Blue Shield that 25% could be saved with hospice care.

Magno found a Washington nursing home that agreed to the hospice experiment and put together a program that cost the patient an average of $140 a day in 1978. Today the cost is $210 a day, about half of what it would cost for a patient in a hospital.

Since then, Magno has started a hospice in Arlington, Va., the suburban Washington community where she lives. Hospices have sprung up all over the country. The number has gone from one in 1973 to 800 today.

There are five hospices or hospice services in the Milwaukee area: St. Joseph's Hospital Hospice, Mount Sinai-Greentree Hospice, and Rogers Memorial Hospice, Oconomowoc; in addition, in-home hospice service is provided by the Visiting Nurse Association and Milwaukee Hospice, Inc.

Insurance coverage for hospice care is a continuing problem. The Southeastern Wisconsin Hospice Council has endorsed home hospice care benefits being built in to health care coverage by employers. Recently, the United Auto Workers regional group in this area endorsed hospice care benefits for all its members. When employers and unions ask for hospice benefits, Blue Cross-Blue Shield will write them into its coverage, according to the hospice council chairman, James Ewens.

It isn't only cost effectiveness, of course, that accounts for the way the hospice movement has exploded in the United States. It is the philosophy of care that has made the quality of life better for the dying.

"A hospice is a concept of care in which the goal is to help a person live until he dies," Magno said. "When the quantity of life is no longer increasing, the quality of life should be at the maximum."

A hospice may be a specific place, such as the nursing home hospice Magno initiated, or it may be support service to families who keep a dying family member at home.

If possible, Magno prefers to see the patient stay at home, she said. Sometimes an inpatient facility is necessary, she explained. There may be a point at which the disease can't be managed at home; perhaps the patient is hemorrhaging or pain control has become difficult. Sometimes the stress of caring for a dying patient is too much for a family and hospital or inpatient hospice care is needed. Those who have no family or whose family cannot provide home care also need inpatient care.

"Always, the question to the patient is, 'What would you rather?' We offer alternatives," said Magno.

When a family and patient have been well informed, they often find they can care very well for the patient at home, Magno said.

"I have only made house calls outside of office hours two or three times. That is because I have explained exactly what to expect and what to do," she said.

This sense of being in command of the situation is an important element of pain control, Magno said.

"A feeling of security is a very good way to control pain. Anxiety intensifies pain," she said.

Five years ago, when the hospice movement was in its infancy, many physicians were hostile to the idea, Magno said.

"Hospice care almost contradicts what we learned in

medical school.

"We were trained to save lives, to prolong life. The hospice says that you can't save this life; the hospice says don't prolong this life.

"We were trained not to mask symptoms; in the hospice we treat symptoms.

"We were trained not to over-use narcotics; the hospice says use as much as necessary to control pain.

"Most physicians consider death a failure. We say it's not a failure, it's the natural end of life," said Magno.

Because of this attitude, doctors and nurses tend to withdraw from dying patients in a hospital, leaving them in isolation. But the hospice aim is to see a patient through death and to include the family in the process.

The three goals of the hospice, Magno said, are to eliminate the pain, loneliness, and loss of control that usually accompany a terminal illness.

Some pain is spiritual, Magno said. She has often prayed with a patient for forgiveness and seen a lessening of pain because of the spiritual peace gained, she said.

"The hospice gives physicians the option of saying, 'I can't cure you, but I can care for you,' " she said.

Lois Blinkhorn

Reprinted with permission from The Milwaukee Journal, October 8, 1981.

CHAPTER THIRTY-TWO

Hospice in America

Hospice in America is still comparatively young. The movement emerged in this country in the early 1970's, and the first U.S. hospice—Hospice, Inc. (now Connecticut Hospice, Inc.), New Haven—opened in 1974. Attempts at evaluation have been limited by the youth of the movement, by its extremely rapid growth, and by its highly individualistic pattern of development. Still, some preliminary assessment can be made about this often poorly understood way of caring for dying patients.

The "hospice movement" is highly diverse. A hospice in a community may mean that some volunteers aid the terminally ill and their families, or that some health professionals in the community are especially interested in the problems of symptom control, or that a special ward of a hospital or even a separate building with a special institutional staff has been designated especially for dying patients. Whatever the setting, however, care is provided in the home when possible, with patients hospitalized only when necessary.

Moreover, the hospice idea in the United States is a transplant. The hospices most familiar to many Americans are English: St. Christopher's or St. Thomas's come quickly to mind. These and other hospices in the United Kingdom are the products of a culture and traditions different from ours. The relationship between institution and society, however, is complicated.

One obvious difference is that Britain has the National Health Service; but hospice did not start in the N.H.S., and many hospices in the U.K. are privately financed. Yet there is a fit between hospice and the British temperament that does not seem to exist in America. The

English G.P. who would never buy a new car, the academic making half the salary of his American colleague these and other segments of the population live their lives a little less insulated from the aches and pains of daily life, from the reality of poverty, suffering, and death than do their American counterparts. The utopian expectation of a discomfort-free life, the streets purged of the ugly and infirm, are not so common. The British ethos has suffered through two wars in ways Americans can't imagine, and it is an ethos in which acceptance of finitude or mortality—the crucial precondition for hospice's success—is more widespread. It's no accident that the British started hospices long before we did.

Furthermore, the N.H.S. is not irrelevant, for Britons have lived for decades with a notion that needed forms of care extend beyond the narrowly physical. Area Health Authorities have responsibility for a broad range of human services and provide an institutional structure, albeit an imperfect one, for coordinating care of the sort that hospice requires. Though there is some balance of power between the center and the periphery in Britain, the N.H.S. nevertheless does provide a mechanism that can be used to encourage a movement like hospice. Inevitably, changes in the philosophy of American medicine will follow a different dynamic.

Defining Hospice

What is the American situation? In 1980, the Joint Commission on Accreditation of Hospitals (J.C.A.H.) surveyed health care agencies across the United States, seeking information on the growth and size of the hospice movement. The survey identified more than 800 programs in various stages of development, some 440 of them functioning. The tally is remarkable when one considers that no hospices at all existed before 1974, and most (51 percent) have begun to offer services to patients only since January 1980. Typically, they are small, with 75 percent admitting fewer than 100 patient/family units in 1980, and only two percent admitting more than 250. The average current caseload was sixteen patient/family units. Sixty percent of the programs reported annual budgets under $75,000; only 10 percent had budgets over $300,000.

Obviously the term "hospice" is broad and vague. Among other things, it denotes a program of care for the dying, a place where such care is provided, or some combination of both. Hospices have sprung up in response to the specific needs of local communities, and an important effect of this heterogeneity is disagreement about goals within the movement itself.

Whatever their size or institutional arrangements, however, hospices share some elements of a common philosophy. It begins with the notion, now a cliche in some circles, that "death is part of life," that there comes a point in medical care when cure is no longer a real possibility and attention must focus on comforting patients and family. This comfort requires relief of symptoms (pain, indigestion, nausea, diarrhea, itching, shortness of breath), and it also involves human social support. Thus hospice forces a redirection of the goals of medicine from cure to palliation, and it implies that medical care must be construed broadly and provided by people with many kinds of skills. Hospice groups necessarily involve people outside the orbit of normal medical practitioners, and misunderstanding or friction between hospice supporters and the medical community is always a possibility.

Before turning to some of the political issues confronting the hospice movement, we should note one problem of perception. For many people hospice means "death house." A visit there is dreaded, and those drawn to it are thought to be morbid. Not only does this image show a failure to understand the philosophy of the hospice movement, which after all does not advocate death, it also is foreign to the reality of hospices, for those institutions fundamentally enhance and improve—

indeed they not infrequently lengthen—life. To the extent that a hospice team succeeds in controlling symptoms, its effect is to make life better. This said, some specific issues should be raised.

Improving the Product

Accreditation and Licensure. At the moment an independent but untrained entrepreneur could simply hang out a shingle and call himself or herself a hospice in all but five states. (Licensing procedures for hospices have been developed by Arizona, Connecticut, Florida, Nevada, and Oregon.) As the benefits of hospice services become more widely known, unscrupulous operators will inevitably exploit the idea. Moreover, some well-intentioned but inferior hospice groups may have unfortunate effects. A community that houses such a hospice may think it is receiving benefits when it is not, and the incentive to develop a good program will be decreased. Under these circumstances it is not surprising that some states have established procedures for licensure and that both the National Hospice Organization (N.H.O., founded in 1978) and the Joint Commission on the Accreditation of Hospitals have taken steps to address the issue of hospice standards.

On the other hand, many presently effective hospices would not meet all the standards that have been proposed by accreditors, and few would meet them in their start-up phase. In other words, accreditation or licensure may inhibit the grass-roots movement, and specific requirements could render some very effective programs illegitimate. This problem occurs whenever a program or service is institutionalized, but the issue here is especially acute because a central part of hospice care is the volunteer in a sense, the amateur— component.

Funding. Hospices have tapped an imaginative list of funding sources, relying heavily on private foundations and community organizations for start-up costs. The

National Cancer Institute has underwritten construction costs and has paid program and evaluation expenses for participants in experimental programs. Recently, a few private insurance carriers have begun to reimburse their policy holders for the costs of hospice care, and hospice costs are included in the benefits packages of a few major corporations (Westinghouse, R.C.A., and General Electric, for example). Congressman Leon Panetta (D.-Calif.) has introduced legislation in the House of Representatives that would allow patients who are eligible for Medicare to obtain services from hospice programs.

To date, however, hospice has not enjoyed large-scale support from the federal government or third-party payers. What coverage there is has been partial and fragmented, largely because of philosphical incompatibilities between hospice and traditional concepts of reimbursable services. Reimbursement policies have been based on a model that seeks the cure of an individual patient who receives skilled services in a health care facility. In contrast, hospice emphasizes the care of patients for whom no cure is possible; it defines the patient and family as the unit of treatment; and, where possible, it seeks to maintain patients in their homes. Moreover, some elements of hospice care can be provided by people with no technical training.

Medicare and Medicaid have provided full reimbursement for hospice services only in pilot or demonstration projects. Partial reimbursement has been available for some relevant care, such as hospital stays, in-patient care in a skilled nursing facility, or nursing visits provided by a certified home health agency. But services such as bereavement and spiritual counseling, homemaker services, and staff education costs have not been reimbursable.

Blue Cross and Blue Shield have endorsed the philosophy of hospice but have asked for assurances of community need, quality, and cost effectiveness in considering reimbursement. In a 1979 Health Services Foundation survey of the sixty-nine Blue Cross and joint Blue Shield Plans, eight of fifty-nine respondents reported full or partial coverage of hospice services. None, however, offered a separate benefit for hospice services.

The lack of support, or ambivalence, of standard funding sources is understandable. Some elements in the movement are wary of outside "help," fearful that accepting support will open the way to outside control. Furthermore, reliable data on the comparative costs of hospice services have been lacking. A project crucial to the future of the movement has been inaugurated by the Health Care Finance Administration (H.C.F.A.), an agency of the U.S. Department of Health and Human Services. Through its national Hospice Demonstration Project, H.C.F.A. has awarded two-year demonstration grants to twenty-six sites in fourteen states. The project seeks information on demand, utilization, cost, and reimbursement policies.

An evaluation of the data generated by the H.C.F.A. project is being done by Brown University. The study, which completed its first annual progress report in June 1981, is seeking answers to the following set of questions:

What is the differential impact of hospice on the quality of life of terminal patients and their families, as compared to "conventional" or customary care?

What are the differential costs of caring for terminally ill patients in hospices and customary care settings?

What is the likely impact of Medicare reimbursement on the organizational structure, staffing pattern, and costs of hospices?

What are the likely national cost implications of reimbursed hospice care?

Developing reliable data is crucial, because it is hard to see how the benefits of hospice can be made widely available without substantial support from federal or third-party financing. Volunteer help is necessary (but not sufficient) for a viable hospice program, which must also involve medical direction, vigorous full-time administration, and skilled nursing services. Even volunteers must be trained. Assuming that we want hospice care to remain something we give to each other, it does not follow that this giving is feasible without some professional assistance and stable funding.

Doctors and Doctoring. While physicians' responses to the hospice movement have been diverse, a few trends are clear. Major medical research centers have not, for the most part, taken a pioneering or even a leading role in developing American hospices, for reasons that are not clear. Their hesitation reflects the lay and reformist character of the American movement and reveals a misfit between the research priorities and incentives of many teaching hospitals and the less dramatic goals of hospice. But the lack of cooperation remains troubling. It reinforces a public image of research medicine that one would like to dismiss as stereotypical, and there is no doubt at all that hospices need skilled medical leadership.

Another problem with doctoring concerns patients who seek hospice care. Should their former physicians hand them over? Should the hospice doctor take charge? In hospices lacking a medical director the issue is moot, but it will become more and more pressing. The attending physician may well be reluctant to let go, perhaps feeling that to do so is to admit defeat or to betray the patient. The patient may not want to offend the doctor. But anyone who has ever worked in a hospice knows how adept at symptom control specialists can become. It's a skill few doctors really have, although there is much they can learn. Unless the pain control specialist has the last medical word, ineffective symptom control will be more common in hospices than is necessary.

The main ideological obstacle stalling the hospice movement in the United States today is the existence of two opposed views: a tendency in the medical community to define the end of medicine as death avoidance and to understand medical art as pure technique, and the tendency of non-professionals to insist that matters of human destiny are nonmedical, so that medical expertise and discussion about them are irrelevant. Both views proceed from the premise that reality is segregated into two realms: the territory of the physician/technician and that of the patient and family. The parties to the argument can never agree about which side is primary, but they share a dualistic perspective that has serious consequences for the hospice movement.

Hospice care can be provided only when health professionals and laypersons work together. If a physician who is an expert at symptom control is not in charge, the patient suffers, for symptom control is not something laymen can accomplish. Symptom control will not appear on the medical agenda, however, unless or until that agenda changes. Changing the agenda is a slow process, perhaps inseparable from broad cultural change, but attempts to short-circuit the process by limiting medical responsibility and asserting the rights of the dying can only impede progress. As John Ladd has remarked in his essay "Legalism and Medical Ethics," the natural territory of rights language is an adversarial relation, and continued reliance on the rhetoric of rights perpetuates an adversarial situation. While this absurd political battle goes on, much unnecessary pain and suffering are added to the human prospect.

The Need for Shared Assumptions

We began this article with reference to the ethical

principles underlying hospice; we attempted to state a common core. But the fact is that struggle over basic principles goes on even within the movement itself. For example, it has often been suggested that hospice units defend an ideal or normative "death trajectory," following the classic Kubler-Ross five stages. The philosophical or religious rationale for this view is not altogether clear. Doubtless it is an important corrective against the denial of death that many have noted in our culture and in our health professions, and, insofar as it enables people to cope with death, it is at least understandable.

On the other hand, critics inside and outside the hospice movement feel that this stance reflects an idealization of death. They contend that long-standing religious and secular traditions in our culture require a more combative attitude toward terminal illness. They worry that a too-easy embrace of hospice will lead to an anti-therapy position. We should neither remove the medical incentive to cure nor reallocate funds so as to discourage the discovery of new cures. And one can defend this more conservative position while still supporting many of the goals of the hospice movement. Obviously it is important to allow individuals the right to refuse hospice care as well as radical surgery. Hospice is not for everyone.

This ongoing argument raises a more fundamental question about the relationship between hospice and personal beliefs. In the U.K., hospices are characteristically rooted in a self-confident and pervasive (if often implicit) religious ethos. There is no great stress on worship or conversion or even belief, but a relaxed trust in widely shared beliefs and loyalties informs most of what is done.

In contrast, the American hospice movement has been Protestant, held together by a rejection of the cure-at-all-cost mind set. But united opposition to a common enemy does not necessarily mean unanimity or agreement on positive principles: Marxists and Reaganites voted against Carter. Can our individual hospices survive without some deeper shared assumptions? Is it possible to undergo the intense suffering that hospice workers experience without community support and a shared set of loyalties? Does a hospice require a philosophy or theology?

This is not to say that hospices can be run only by "true believers." But any observer of hospices notices some things. In hospices the patients and doctors have limited powers; they have plans, but the striking fact is how often their plans must be revised. They wonder about what they should do and who they are; they find themselves struggling to cope. The problem they face is not how to get rid of dependencies but how to resolve conflicting ties and learn to live with dependency. The hospice patient can be autonomous in an important sense of that word; dignity and thinking for himself do matter. But the overwhelming fact of his life, and of the lives of those who provide him with care, is his dependence on or relatedness to others. Debilitating illness makes it impossible not to come to terms with this fact.

The hard issue is what status the philosopher in each of us will accord the hospice patient. Does this weakened, suffering individual represent an aberration, the kind of human fate that should be avoided at all cost? Does he or she represent a failure of selfhood and of a society that can allow weakness and dependency?

Our sense is the opposite: that he or she represents a paradigm of the human condition. As the infant shows us what we have all come from, the hospice patient shows us that to which we all are destined. That is the most important moral lesson of hospices. We do not have the possibility of omnipotence, and we cannot always keep our hands clean. Hospice experience suggests: to be human is to take responsibility for each other and to allow ourselves to be helped.

David H. Smith and Judith A. Granbois

CHAPTER THIRTY-THREE

The Evolution of a Hospice

In reading through the increasing numbers of articles dealing with the hospice concept, I have been struck by the almost universal characterization of hospice as an ideal service. The case material cited as testimony to the success of hospices would make a public relations agent blush. I was tempted to wonder, "Death, where is thy sting?"

The unsettling mystique surrounding "hospice" begins with the word itself. Almost every article provides an historical description of hospice as a refuge where pilgrims and crusaders on their religious and military journeys could rest and/or be tended by religiously motivated groups. This allusion to past times evokes an ethereal sense of well-being—the weary sojourner being tended by devoted caretakers—but does this image fit the modern hospice? Yes and no.

Most hospice services are provided in the homes of dying people, which alters the metaphor considerably. Unlike the ancient systems, home hospice teams (professionals and volunteers) journey to the pilgrims and crusaders, not vice versa. Care is offered not in a homogeneous institution, but in a dynamic, hetero-geneous family setting, with multiple motivations. In the modern home hospice, which I will later describe in detail, a sense of well-being proceeds from two sources: family and hospice team. Either can influence the outcome decisively.

Just as each family presents a unique context for care, so does each hospice service. Programs differ widely as to the services they provide, the fees they charge or don't charge, and their philosophical motivations. For example, some programs consist strictly of volunteers who provide supportive visits and may attempt to coordinate existing community services in nursing, social work, and so forth. Others provide all the services designated by the National Hospice Organization (N.H.O.) as essential in the definition of hospice. In actual practice the resulting difference might look something like this:

A program coordinator from Hospice A, an all-volunteer program, meets with the patient and the Jones family and sets up a visiting schedule for a volunteer. The coordinator also contacts a local nursing service, which will consult with the attending physician before providing its own service to the family. Communication is established between the volunteer and the nurse in an attempt to offer a coordinated approach. However, the hospice program coordinator has no authority over the nurses.

Hospice B is an all-inclusive service that employs nurses, social workers, volunteers, and aides. Their program coordinator meets with the patient and the Jones family to develop a plan of care in consultation with the attending physician. The program coordinator has authority over all hospice services. In the course of the interview, she learns that the patient is under sixty-five and carries insurance that covers only 80 percent of nursing service. Since no funds are available to cover the remaining 20 percent, the problem of reimbursement arises.

From this limited example, several clear differences emerge. Hospice A does not have a single, centralized authority for all services. Hospice B does. Hospice A does not need to worry about payments in order to survive (the hospice doesn't, but the nursing service may, and some community services do not provide free services when reimbursement is not available). Hospice B, however, is confronted with a choice about financing care. Should the hospice waive payment, negotiate a deferred payment plan, limit service, or refuse care altogether? The delicacy of this situation cannot be stressed enough, since good hospice care depends on developing a trusting relationship with the family.

The differing perspectives of Hospice A and Hospice B will influence care, approaches, and outcomes. Hospice A, the all-volunteer coordinating agency, can be 100 percent idealistic in its approach because it does not seek any reimbursement for its services. There is no possibility of alienation on financial grounds. However, Hospice B, which pays salaries and benefits to its employees, must seek reimbursement. Financial realities will temper idealism in this instance and can create friction between the hospice and family.

Both organizational structures have their advantages and disadvantages. While Hospice A, with its volunteer services, may operate along purely altruistic lines, it cannot insist on conformity from the paid community services it attempts to coordinate. On the other hand, Hospice B, which must make a thorough assessment of family resources, can enforce policy within the team and insure uniformity of services. Such differences can have a marked impact on the family's experience.

Existing literature teems with illustrations of harmonious interactions between knowledgeable hospice teams and grateful families. Indeed, there is hardly a mention of doubts, conflicts, or stress. When problems are cited, the family has them; the hospice team holds the solutions. It is a portrait of magic. But is it real? Only sometimes. Success, by which I mean the relative sense of well-being felt by the dying person and the family, is directly attributable to the level of mutual respect and cooperation between family and service. Without trust, hospice is meaningless, but the relationship is rarely ideal. Too often hospice care suffers from the same societal ills that plague other enterprises: over-professionalization, over-servicing, the sapping of family strength, and the thorny issues of ethics and economics that influence care for the terminally ill.

Consider an initial meeting with the family. The patient's wife answers the door in a bathrobe at 3:00 p.m. The house is messy. Several family members are trying, rather clumsily, to change the patient's bedding. Everyone seems tense and is somewhat reluctant to enter a discussion with the "visitor." How the team evaluates this scene will have tremendous impact on the progress of the case. If the hospice team member responds judgmentally to the appearance of chaos he or she may decide that the family is inadequate in giving care. As a result, the interview may be structured to convince the family that they need more professional help, such as an aide. If the family feels inadequate, which is often the case, they may welcome the offer of an aide, only to feel displaced later on.

If that happens, the initial assessment—though well intentioned—has defeated the very role of hospice: helping the family care for itself. The initial assessment of the family can also be influenced by the hospice's organizational structure, since the team member conducts the assessment according to program design. If the hospice is all-volunteer, the goal becomes placing a volunteer; if the hospice offers "full service," the family's resources will be assessed. In either case, the possibility exists that the needs of the hospice may predominate. The hospice then becomes the opposite of what was intended: an institution that oppresses families and lessens their freedom of choice.

An "Ideal" Beginning

Two years ago the Visiting Nurse Association (V.N.A.) of Evanston, Illinois, faced some of these issues when it embarked on a project to provide home hospice care for terminally ill patients. This is a brief account of the evolution of that project, which involved a shift in attention from imagined ideals to real practice, and from the professional to the family. The family was initially defined as the object of care, but family members later proved to be the primary hospice workers as well.

Since 1976 requests for help with dying patients had been growing steadily, and the nursing agency realized that under circumstances of imminent death, complicated patient and family needs called for services beyond the usual scope. Admission criteria to the new program were loosely defined: the patient had to suffer from a life-threatening disease and live within a particular geographic area to receive service. The goal was to insure a dignified, comfortable death at home.

In the planning phase during 1979 the Terminal Care Project (T.C.P.) set out to develop a package of services that would take the sting out of death. Originally three agencies collaborated to provide a full spectrum of services for families with dying members. A community-based counseling agency supplied social work services. A local mental health organization recruited and trained a core group of ten volunteers. The V.N.A. provided nursing and other health services, and was responsible for financial and administrative functions. Though V.N.A. had obtained the grant that funded the project, it was not clearly designated as the lead agency. Cooperation was part of the program's ideal assumption, and so lines of authority were never established.

Thanks to adequate funding, the staffs of the three agencies participated in an eight-week orientation program conducted by a consulting psychologist. The teams attempted to set a single standard of care for patients and their families, but their assessments of the families' needs were never reviewed by a supervisor. Therefore, the plans that were put into effect, including fee adjustments and placements of personnel, were only as effective as the individual teams.

Once care was underway, the teams continued meeting weekly. The meetings had a dual purpose: they aimed at continuity of care and adequate communication among team members. However, because there was no designated leader with the authority to set policy, control the budget, and have the final word on service placements, the most vocal team member exerted the greatest influence. This situation created resentments and rivalries, with team members banding together by discipline—the social workers versus the nurses, the nurses versus the health aides, and so on.

With no recourse for settling disputes along policy lines, the intra-team competition sometimes spilled over and inadvertently influenced the patient and family. When families sensed that the helpers were divided, they grew more insecure and often requested—even demanded—more service. As a client survey demonstrated, team problems can create ineffective service and result in added costs.

The Awakening

Eight months into the initial phase of the program, a client survey was taken. The survey asked the patients and their families whether they had been satisfied with the service and what additional care they might have needed. Seventy surveys were sent, forty were returned. Requests for further service included: home health aides for longer periods of time; more intensive emotional supports from social workers, clergymen, or volunteers; transportation; and individual or group counseling during the bereavement period.

On the basis of the survey and the staff's experiences in giving care, the administration of the V.N.A. set out to design the second phase of the program. But questions surfaced that had not been anticipated. To begin with, the cooperative multi-agency approach was beginning to wear thin. The hospice fabric was being stretched to clothe competing professional agendas and the little black bag was stuffed with an endless array of things to "do" for clients that nobody would or should pay for.

The staff also began to worry that the project was becoming a part of the death industry. The services family members cited as lacking or inadequate were the kinds of care that most families, with some guidance or encouragement, could provide for themselves; yet they wanted professionals to do the job. Though the staff members never questioned that the hospice concept was good and necessary, they were beginning to realize that hospice works best when the family and the hospice team confront the frightening reality of death together. That is the magic.

The realization that families, not the hospice team, were the real primary hospice workers, and that competing professional disciplines could make the work more difficult for those families, shaped the agenda for the second year of hospice, at least as far as this group was concerned.

If the family is to carry the bulk of hospice work, how do we decide the role of the hospice team and how will the real world approximate the ideal? The answer to the first question is simple: hospice workers should help the family to realize their potential in caring for the dying person and for each other, and they should try within reason to do whatever the family cannot accomplish. In keeping with this guideline, the family assumes the prime responsibility for its own fate, with hospice team members as valuable resources to draw on.

In answering the second question—that of the relation between practice and ideal—two things must be understood. First, home hospice services enter already established family systems that have functioned more or less successfully for years. Second, a team entering a home is dramatically different from a family entering an institution. The characteristics of different families will determine how closely the real approximates the ideal. Prominent among these characteristics are the physical and psychological needs of the patient; the degree of intimacy in family relationships; the numbers, availability, and willingness to help of nuclear and extended family; the psychological sophistication of various members; the physical health of caretakers; previous experiences with illnesses and death; economic resources; ethical and religious convictions; coping skills; and the permeability of the family system to outside resources. The quantity and quality of service will depend on the various levels and combinations of these characteristics. Therefore, the initial assessment of the family becomes crucial, not only in defining the pattern of the service, but also in setting the tone of the relationship.

To make families more self-reliant, the key factors are respect, restraint, cooperation, and flexibility. Often a well-intentioned hospice can cripple a family in its effort to care for its dying member. The deluge of service resulting from a careless assessment may relieve a crisis atmosphere, but it can also produce a quiet sense of helplessness and depression in a family stripped of responsibility and need to care for its own.

This error, which may engender feelings of inadequacy in the family, can lead after the patient's death to prolonged and serious grief and mourning. The hospice team and the family must develop their plans together in an atmosphere of mutual respect. The team must exercise restraint, never assuming that the family needs every hospice service, and ultimately the family must have veto power over services offered. Professional agendas and ideals must never be imposed on families. The plan of care should be fully worked out, yet flexible.

Certainly some families inappropriately assess their own needs and capabilities, and when that happens the hospice team should try to counter any distortion. However, even then they should recognize that more often than not people die as they have lived and it is not the role of hospice to insure transformation of less-than-perfect families.

A case on which I worked illustrates the difficult
interplay in developing plans with families. A patient,
let us call him Tom Ellison, age sixty-seven, was
completely bedridden with metastatic prostate cancer
and partial paralysis from a stroke. His family background included a long history of disturbed relationships. His wife, who worked full time, chose to
shoulder nearly all of the physical care of her husband.
His children, both young adults living at home, though
capable of contributing care, remained unmoved and
uninvolved. Ellison, determined to be at home, had left
the hospital against medical advice and refused a
nursing home placement. Both he and his family refused
to hire help that would insure his safety during working
hours. They would accept only one and a half to two
hours of daily nursing care. Volunteer assistance and
family counseling were both refused. Hospice was
viewed by the family not as an ideal group, but as a
necessary intrusion that would provide services they
simply had to have for minimum safety.

In this situation, our hospice team confronted several
critical issues: patient safety, family self-determina-
tion, and reimbursement. In assessing the risks of
leaving the patient alone, we felt very uneasy and
wondered whether or not to provide the limited service
that the family had requested. However, we decided to
proceed day by day and work toward various goals:
involving other family members, adding aide coverage
during working hours, and placing a volunteer. We felt
the patient's condition warranted daily skilled nursing
care but were fully aware that Medicare might decide
otherwise, which would precipitate a financial crisis for
the hospice and the family. As the case progressed, we
made some headway in all areas. The children and other
family members became minimally involved, the family
agreed to accept an aide four hours daily through a
state-funded program, and we placed a volunteer one
day a week to help with household tasks and support

Mrs. Ellison, whose emotional stress steadily increased. Medicare questioned the claim for the nurse, but after some discussion agreed to reimburse the costs. Despite all the resources of hospice, however, the family never attained the ideal of hospice. Hospice can offer services that promote death with dignity, but it cannot insist on or guarantee the outcome.

Surmounting Obstacles

Determining the services a family needs, their frequency, and their costs can be an agonizing process. As this case demonstrates, the patient's and family's needs do not always emerge clearly. Program constraints such as staff time, nonreimbursed costs, and administrative requirements play a hidden but influential role in determining what services can be offered. The best way to deal with these conflicts is to have frank discussions with families about limited resources and encourage them to provide services for themselves. Families can be helped to organize themselves, to locate and set up equipment, to mobilize extended family or neighbors, and to develop patterns of family staffing. They can be instructed in hands-on care where unskilled services are sufficient. They can be assisted with financial questions: what community resources are available; how best to reallocate family finances; and how to understand and utilize third party resources, such as insurance, Medicare, or Medicaid. Consistent, ongoing monitoring of the situation will allow hospice workers to intervene when necessary. Meanwhile, the family develops the sense that someone is always available to help.

Making the family aware from the start of real issues and real limitations will prevent disappointments and broken promises later on. From experience with nearly 300 families over two and a half years, the Evanston V.N.A. concluded that the ability of the patient and family to make informed decisions is the foundation of a sound and cost-effective therapeutic service.

In order to provide better hospice care, the V.N.A. made several organizational changes. First, they decided that all services would originate from the V.N.A. By centralizing service, the hospice effectively cut through competing professional agendas and avoided bureaucratic snags. Second, they appointed a leader. This full-time director, a social worker, shares the perception of the V.N.A. administration. He has an extensive background in family systems and program administration, and was made responsible for coordinating the hospice team, collecting and analyzing data, heightening public awareness of the service, managing the budget, approving service placements, and directing clinical social work services. Third, criteria for admission to the program were sharpened to include an approximate life expectancy of three months (now extended to six months); an awareness of the prognosis by the patient and family; support from the physician for hospice care; and compliance with geographical limits.

These changes have led to a better and more consistent quality of service, reduced cost for families and the agency, and better emotional adjustment for everyone concerned. In addition, when the costs of home hospice care are compared with average daily hospital costs in the nearby Chicago area, the cost-effectiveness factor becomes even more obvious. For hospital bed space alone the average daily cost is $240. In 1979 V.N.A. full home hospice care cost $34 per day; by 1980 daily costs were reduced to $22.

The ancient hospice has cast a romantic shadow on its modern-day counterpart. Of course, early hospices had their economic and emotional struggles too, but with time these have been forgotten. Only when we look at the functioning hospice do the practical difficulties emerge. Every family is unique and each calls for individual attention. Respect, restraint, flexibility, and cooperation—these are the bywords of effective hospice care. Because of the real limitations—human and financial—in caring for dying people, total comfort is an ideal to be passionately pursued, but no one should promise that the outcome will be perfect.

Peter Mudd

This article originally appeared in <u>The</u> <u>Hastings</u> <u>Center</u> <u>Report</u>, April 1982.

CHAPTER THIRTY-FOUR

Suggested Readings

The Royal Victoria Hospital Manual On Palliative Hospice Care: A Resource Book. Edited by Ina Ajemian and Balfour Mount. New York: Arno Press, 1980.

Death: The Final Stage of Growth by Elisabeth Kubler-Ross. Englewood Cliffs, N.J.: Prentice-Hall, Inc., 1975.

First American Hospice: Three Years of Home Care by Sylvia Lack and Robert Buckingham. New Haven: Hospice of Connecticut. 1978.

Mother Teresa: Her People and Her Work by Desmond Doig. New York: Harper & Row, Publishers, 1976.

Care of the Dying by Cicely Saunders, M.D. London: Macmillan and Company Limited, 1959.

A Guide to Dying At Home by Deborah Duda. Santa Fe: John Muir Publications, 1982.

Original
Blessing

Original Blessing
the primer in creation spirituality
A new book by Matthew Fox, op

The basics of creation spirituality in succinct, easy-to-read, yet scholarly supported fashion.

At an introductory price of $8.95

Structured around Meister Eckhart's four paths the book is divided into four sections: BEFRIENDING CREATION; Letting Go and Letting Be (Befriending Darkness); BEFRIENDING OUR DIVINITY, OUR CREATIVITY; The New Creation: Compassion and Social Justice.

Matthew Fox's newest and best!

Chapters include: CREATION AS BLESSING; our earthiness as a blessing; OUR ROYAL PERSONHOOD; touching pain; THE EXPERIENCE OF NOTHINGNESS; the emptiness that precedes birthing; DISCIPLINE — YES! ASCETICISM — NO!; becoming a prophet; COMPASSION AS PASSION FOR JUSTICE; for celebration, joy and humor; THE SPIRITUALITY OF THE OPPRESSED; some applications of creation spirituality to transforming western religion and theology— feminism, the Christ, the four paths and salvation, transforming western culture...

0-939680-07-6 264 pages **$8.95**

Original Blessing by Matt Fox, the author of WHEE, We, wee All the Way Home, Compassion, Breakthrough, Musical Mystical Bear, Western Spirituality and other great books!

SYMBION

A Glimpse into the future...
Spirituality for a possible future
by Richard Woods

A daring series of explorations in spirituality as a way toward a possible, better future...

In his latest book, Richard Woods, OP examines various elements and aspects of contemporary experiences, both problems and promises, in a view of trends already bearing us along some startling trajectories.

Symbion explores a mysticism for the future — ordinary mysticism, integration, the social dimension of religious experience, ecological sensitivity.

Symbion by Richard Woods

0-939680-08-4 264 pages **$8.95**

The Captain America Complex

Spirituality and the political paths of our times...
by Robert Jewett

"Provides a discerning examination of America's national soul."
— SENATOR MARK HATFIELD

The Captain America Complex is a fair-minded, carefully documented, yet highly readable study about one of the most **scripture-based**, political paths of our time. Neither an attack or an apology. Christian in a very real sense. Valuable reading not only for those who seek witness in politics but for those seeking/searching for a refreshing look at government and politics **through Christ-colored glasses.**

The Captain American Complex

0-939680-09-2 264 pages **$8.95**

WHEE, We, wee
All the Way Home

Another Classic by Matthew Fox
A Guide to a sensual prophetic spirituality
with a brand new introduction to the 80's

by Matthew Fox, op

"This book has excitement, color, swiftness and is
service to the Church. WHEE! is a book for searchers
into the meaning of life and revelation."
— Review for Religious

"WHEE! is provocative, exciting, and radical both in
its scope and ideas. It is both socially relevant and
psychologically sound." — Library Journal

0-939680-00-9 224 pages **$8.95**

MANIFESTO
for a Global Civilization

Matthew Fox, theologian and Brian Swimme, physicist collaborate in . . .

Explore the connection between the universe and
our Christian spirituality with Matthew Fox and Dr.
Brian Swimme in this dialogue of a vision to save
the world for the beautiful. In a world of chaos,
confusion and mistrust Matt Fox and Brian
Swimme show us a vision of hope which will
enable us to center our experience of the here
and now into redeeming the world.

Perfect for group discussion.

0939680-05-X **$3.50**

Meditations with™

A FEW WORDS WITH MATTHEW FOX, O.P.

"Bear & Company is publishing this series of creation-centered mystic/prophets to bring to the attention and prayer of peoples today the power and energy of the holistic mystics of the western tradition. One reason western culture succumbs to boredom and to violence is that we are not being challenged by our religious traditions to be all we can be. This is also the reason that many sincere spiritual seekers go East for their mysticism — because the West is itself out of touch with its deepest spiritual guides.

Meditations with™ Meister Eckhart
by Matthew Fox

For Eckhart to be spiritual is to be awake and alive — Creation itself is sacrament. The spiritual life begins where life does — "the spring of life...the heart."

Reflections of Meister Eckhart with an introduction and versions by Matthew Fox.

"Spirituality begins with humanity's potential to act divinely in the ways of beauty-making, compassion, and sharing."

0-939680-04-1 128 pages **$6.95 with ART**

Meditations with™ Julian of Norwich
by Brendan Doyle
with foreword by Patricia Vinje
and preface by Matthew Fox

Julian's spirituality is based in acknowledging God where God is. Her creation-centered vision — God-with-in-us — was the basis of her meditation. Brendan Doyle presents this feminist mystic's words in the context of her capacity to find meaning in creation. A treasure house for meditative reading.

0-939680-11-4 128 pages **$6.95 with ART**

Meditions with™
Hildegarde of Bingen

by Gabriele Uhlein
with foreword by Thomas Berry and
Preface by Matthew Fox

Sharings from the 26 "visions" of this ageless
Benedictine of Medieval Germany. Visions which
this "new age," this age of alternative, holistic
spiritualities is at ease with. From this famous
Benedictine sharings of her 26 "visions"...

Gabriele Uhlein selected these messages from a
woman of profound prayer and insight—
Hildegarde of Bingen.

0-939680-12-2 128 pages **$6.95 with ART**

Meditations with™
Mechtild   of Magdeburg

by Sue Woodruff
Foreword by Matthew Fox

Like so many women of the middle ages
Mechtild was a prophet who loudly decried the
abuses of organized religions and its priests in her
day. While she made enemies this way, she did
not cease composing this beautiful poetry of the
soul for those who live very much in the world.

In this book, the author, Sue Woodruff, brings
together, in moving drawings, and well chosen
verse from Mechtild a beautiful meditation
experience—one based in God's beauty in
creation, and humanity's dignity in God.

0-939680-08-8 128 pages **$6.95 with ART**

TAPES BY MATTHEW FOX AND FRIENDS

One of the country's most popular retreat masters and spiritual guides has prepared an extraordinary cassette program.

+ MATTHEW FOX has prepared 15 complete tape programs rooted in a vision of a prayer life that has its flower in compassionate caring.

+ Jose Hobday, Msgr Robert Fox, Brian Swimme, MATT and other friends share their experience, strength and hope with you.

+ Spend a weekend with them . . . stretch them over days or weeks

+ Use them at home . . . lone, in a group . . . in a classroom, or in your car.

+ A fresh, imaginative, prayer resource you've been waiting for.

JUST RELEASED!

TAPE 15: Spirituality and Education

In this tape Matt Fox shares his insights into a Creation-Centered approach to education. He draws from his experiences as teacher/learner. He discounts the "Jacob's ladder approach to education as doing something to another or superior/inferior relationships. He demonstrates concrete ways in which teachers and "students" can dance "Sarah's Circle" of compassion, caring, wisdom and inter-dependence. The discipline of reverencing life constitutes the heart of all human learning.

TAPE 14: Science, Spirituality and Education

Matt Fox dialogues with physicist/mathematician Dr. Brian Swimme in exploring the connection between the Mysteries of the Universe and Our Christian Spirituality. They describe their MANIFESTO (see this catalogue) for a global community. A renewed spirituality will allow a dialogue of science, education, and culture if religious faith will not seek its own perpetuation but will believe deeply enough that it can let go of its own privileged positions in order to be among the least and the poorest.

TAPE EIGHT: Holiness as Cosmic Hospitality

Pointing out that the meaning of holiness must be sought for our time. The theological explanation of hospitality, God as host/hostess, and the practical ramifications of hospitality to *self, others, nature and God*.

TAPE SEVEN: Images of Soul: psychology of spirituality

A terminal case of "left-brain-itis" haunts western civilization. Words have lost their moorings and meanings. Philosopher Charles Fair points out that when a civilization looses its meaning of "soul" that civilization dies. Today, in the west, we have lost the meaning of soul and we need to return to "right-brain" insights for soul. These are expressed by images—out of new images of soul a new civilization can be born. Special attention is given to Meister Eckhart's images of soul.

TAPE SIX: Recovering Ritual in the West: liturgy & spirituality

A look at liturgy, music and ritual. An analysis of what's wrong in the west plus antidotes for healing. This analysis includes the absence of cosmos, body, social justice, and via negativa when westerners gather to worship. Antidotes for healing this malaise are noted with special attention paid to the prophetic role of music.

TAPE 13: Body as Metaphor

Jungian Analyst John Giannini and Matt Fox discuss the recovery of the holy trinity of Body, Soul, and Spirit. Eckhardt's wholistic, cosmic spirituality and Jung's principle of synchronicity heal the microcosm and macrocosm of western consciousness torn asunder by an ascetic dualism that pits spirit against matter.

TAPE 12: Creativity & Spirituality—a trialogue with Jose Hobday, Msgr. Robert Fox, and Matthew Fox. Street Priest, Msgr. Robert Fox of Harlem shares his experience of a creation-centered spirituality on the streets of New York. All three share that finding God in the midst of life is finding yourself, your neighbor, and all of creation and believing "it is good."

TAPE 11: An American Spirituality

Matt Fox believes that the phenomenon of prayer and interest in adult spirituality is clearly at the forefront of American culture today. In this tape he presents the forms this phenomenon takes and some of the reasons "why" we should not be surprised. Prayer as a cover up for injustice is dead. The quest of the American spirituality may be to end the CHAOS.

TAPE 10: A Native American Spirituality

Native American, Sister Jose Hobday dialogues with Matt Fox regarding the creation-centered tradition of the Native American Spirituality. Explored are images of soul, community, and person.

TAPE NINE: Social Justice, Art & Spirituality: a Holy Trinity and indivisible unity

Part and parcel of every unjust system is the separation of justice and art. Such separation renders art as mere entertainment or as investment for the powerful. Yet art remains the meaningful link between theory and social change; and between personal transformation & social transformation. This tape explores bringing the trinity of social justice, art and spirituality together again.

TAPE FIVE: Pleasure, Contemplation and Social Justice: antidote to the idolatry of consumerism

This meaning of contemplation as pleasure and savoring contemplation. This meaning of contemplation as pleasure and savoring contemplation . . . One reason why consumerism has taken such deep root in western culture is that western spiritualities have too often ignored a theology of pleasure. The Holy Spirit is discovered as the "Spirit of Transformation."

TAPE FOUR: Images of Compassion: East meets West

It seems that when you get to the roots of all major world spiritual traditions, they are all trying to teach people compassion. This tape examines four images found in all world religions to educate in compassion.

TAPE THREE: Psychology & Mysticism—Jung & Meister Eckhart

Jung admits his dependence on the great Dominican mystic Meister Eckhart when he writes that reading Meister Eckhart gave him "the key" to opening up the unconscious. This tape examines the insights into the human spirit uncovered by Meister Eckhart and Carl Gustave Jung; the importance of matter in our spiritual life.

TAPE TWO: Family Spirituality

The 1980's have been declared the decade of the family. This reflection considers three dimensions to family and spirituality: 1) The meaning of family with special attention to the cosmic family or "family of being" of which biblical tradition teaches; 2) Our family or local unit of intimacy as mystical energy source—family as celebration; and 3) Our family or local unit of intimacy as a prophetic energy—the family as a resistance unit.

TAPE ONE: From Climbing Jacob's Ladder to Dancing Sarah's Circle

A reflection on the change in mystical symbols from the overly competitive and self-centered "climbing Jacob's ladder" to the symbol of interdependence, creativity, humor and gentle living characterized by "Sarah's Circle."

THE HOSPICE HANDBOOK

Helping...Healing...
by Jim Ewens and Patricia Herrington of
the Milwaukee Hospice

"This book contains much practical information..." — Elisabeth Kubler-Ross

THE handbook for those who wish to participate in
this prophetic compassionate movement of the
1980's. Jim, Pat and the Milwaukee Hospice
Community share their experience, strength and
hope in caring for hospice patients and their
"families." Sensitive photography by Don Doll, SJ
enhances the presentation.

Sections include: "FAMILY"; Questions on Hospice
Care; REFLECTIONS FROM FAMILIES; Helping
Children; SUPPORT SYSTEMS; Legal Considerations;
FUNERAL ARRANGEMENTS; Aspects of Grieving;
SPIRITUAL CARE; and, Information for Hospice.

**HOSPICE: a handbook for families and others
facing terminal illness.**

0-939680-10-6.244 pages, photography **$8.95**

PSALMS FROM THE HILLS
OF WEST VIRGINIA

by Janet Hurlow with introduction by
Matthew Fox, op

Can a simple and good mountain lady, poorer in
this world's goods than the vast majority of
Americans have a prosperity to share that even the
richest among us crave?

Psalms from the Hills of West Virginia announces the
Glad Tidings of old that have been so often
muddled over.

Inspirations for the prayer-life of creation-centered
people. Good for personal and group prayer and
reflection.

0-9399680-02-5 144 pages **$8.95**

Qty	ORDER FORM	Each	Total
	Bear & Company "little magazine"	$30.00	
	CANADIAN ORDERS: ADD $6.00 FOR PROCESSING		
	TAPE ONE: Climbing/Dancing	7.95	
	TAPE TWO: Family Spirituality	7.95	
	TAPE THREE: Psychology & Mysticism	7.95	
	TAPE FOUR: Images of Compassion	7.95	
	TAPE FIVE: Pleasure, Contemplation, Justice	7.95	
	TAPE SIX: Recovering Ritual	7.95	
	TAPE SEVEN: Images of Soul	7.95	
	TAPE EIGHT: Holiness Cosmic Hospitality	7.95	
	TAPE NINE: Social Justice, ART, Spirituality	7.95	
	TAPE 10: A Native American Spirituality	7.95	
	TAPE 11: An American Spirituality	7.95	
	TAPE 12: A Spirituality for the Streets	7.95	
	TAPE 13: Body as Metaphor	7.95	
	TAPE 14: Science, Spirituality & Education	7.95	
	TAPE 15: Spirituality & Education	7.95	
	Cash Total Tapes		
	TOTAL TAPES & BOOKS		
	10% Handling & Shipping		
	TOTAL		

ALL MONIES MUST BE IN U.S. FUNDS ONLY
PAYABLE THROUGH A CONTINENTAL U.S. BANK

Check   Money Order   Visa   Mastercard

NAME _____

STREET _____

CITY _____ STATE _____ ZIP ___

Card Number _____ Expires ___

Signature _____

MAIL YOUR ORDER TODAY TO: BEAR & COMPANY, INC.

PO DRAWER 2860   SANTA FE, NEW MEXICO 87504-2860

Bear and Company, Inc.

publishes a complete line of creation centered spirituality materials by Matt Fox and associates.

+   Fine Books including: Whee! We, wee
                                           Western Spirituality

+   A "little magazine" :   Bear & Company

+   Program materials including cassette
        tapes & spirit masters.

Order from your local bookstore. For the location of the store nearest you featuring Bear & Company or for a complete catalog please fill out this form or call (505) 983-5968.

To: Bear & Company, Inc.
       PO DRAWER 2860
       SANTA FE, NEW MEXICO 87504-2860

Send to: _____

Street _____

City/State _____Zip _____

☐   Please send me a catalog

☐   Put me on your mailing list

☐   Which store in my area carries Bear & Company materials

☐   I am interested in your "little Magazine"

☐   I am interested in program materials